CONTENTS

ACKNOWLEDGEMENTS

Writing this book has been a journey—one that wouldn't have been possible without the love, encouragement, and inspiration I've received along the way.

To my best half, Mukta—thank you for your unwavering support. I wanted to keep this book a secret until it was complete, but you saw right through me. When you guessed what I was up to, it only pushed me forward. Thank you for listening to every chapter, for your patience, and for always being there. This book is as much yours as it is mine.

To my family—thank you for tolerating my countless excuses about not telling you I was writing a book. To my Aai and Baba, for reminding me that whatever I do, I should always strive to be a good and kind human being. To my elder brother, Sumeet—DADA as I call him—thank you for being my guide, my anchor, and always looking out for me. To my sister-in-law, Prajakta, who has treated me like her own brother and supported me unconditionally. To my nephew, Raghaveer, who sees me more as a friend than an uncle—and sometimes, an older brother. And to my daughter, Ira, my greatest source of strength and motivation. She may treat me like her child, but it's this child who happily carries all her tantrums.

To my friends, coworkers, and the countless strangers I have met along the way—those from road trips, chance encounters, and everyday interactions. You've shared your experiences, your wisdom, and your happiness with me in ways you may not even realize. Without those moments, this book wouldn't exist. A special shoutout to my coffee, my helmet, my video games, and my musical instruments—for giving me the quiet spaces where I could think, reflect, and create.

A heartfelt thank you to Mr. Atul Kahate—my teacher, a mentor, and a renowned author—who inspired me to write long before I even considered it. Thank you for reading my work and offering your valuable insights. It means the world to me.

To my editors and publishers—thank you for your keen attention to detail, for believing in my vision, and for shaping this book into what it is today.

And finally, to those I have yet to meet, and even those who are yet to be born—you will bring new lessons, new perspectives, and new joys into my life. I look forward to them all.

To everyone who has been part of this journey—thank you for being a reason for my happiness. Stay happy, and make the world a little happier, one moment at a time.

Yours,
– Saket

HAPPINESS IS ALWAYS WITHIN AND AROUND

SIMPLE PRACTICES TO BE FOLLOWED TO REINVENT LASTING HAPPINESS

SAKET SHASHIKANT PATRIKAR

ISBN
Paperback 979-8-89724-947-3
Hardcase 979-8-89744-966-8

ABOUT THE AUTHOR

Saket Shashikant Patrikar is a technologist by profession and an artist at heart. He ensures product quality in his work but is equally passionate about the quality of life. An avid explorer of human psychology and behavioral science, believing that happiness is something we create, not something we wait for.

Raised in a joint family, Saket grew up with strong values of empathy and meaningful connections. While pursuing higher studies in Pune, he found another form of family in friendships, reinforcing his belief in the power of relationships to shape happiness.

Music, books, and movies have been lifelong influences. Music, in particular, transformed his journey, even leading him to be a record holder by participating in a Guinness World Record event. Books deepened his self-awareness and passion for personal growth, strengthening his belief that change starts from within.

His work in product quality inspired a realization—life's quality is measured by the happiness we cultivate. This perspective led him to study human behavior, offer stress management sessions, and now, write this book.

During the COVID-19 pandemic, he refined his observations and began sharing techniques to help people manage stress and build a more fulfilling life. The experience reinforced his belief that happiness is universal and within reach.

Saket enjoys meeting new people, learning from their stories, and understanding the different ways individuals find joy. This book is a culmination of those experiences, offering insights and practical tools to help others shape their own happiness. His goal is simple—to spread happiness and remind people that joy is always within reach, often in the simplest moments of life.

PREFACE

"Happiness is a warm puppy," said Charles Schulz.

But if you're like most of us, you probably don't have a puppy curled up by your side. Instead, your days are filled with work deadlines, family obligations, and an endless stream of notifications pulling you in every direction. Somewhere along the way, happiness stopped feeling warm—it became another task, buried beneath the weight of everything you need to get done and cross off your never-ending to-do list.

And yet, every so often, something simple breaks through. Maybe you catch a glimpse of a child laughing with their parents over a silly joke, or you hear a familiar song that takes you back to a lighter time. For a brief moment, everything else fades. It feels uncomplicated, natural, and pure. But then, just as quickly, the moment slips away, leaving you wondering: why doesn't it last?

Happiness is such a simple idea, yet it carries an entire lifetime's meaning.

For some, it's the rush of a new accomplishment. For others, it's found in quiet moments of contentment. Across generations, cultures, and circumstances, its essence has shifted, shaped by changing expectations and values. It has been tied to the things we own, the people we love, and the milestones we achieve. But regardless of how each of us defines it, one truth remains constant: we all long for it.

And yet, it feels harder to hold onto than ever before. Life is full of distractions—endless notifications, the pressure to keep up, responsibilities, and constant comparisons all diminish the small joys we could enjoy. We've been so focused on chasing happiness like a prize at the end of a race that we've forgotten to notice it in the moments around us.

This book was born from the realization that we've made happiness more complicated than it needs to be. Over time, we've added layers of expectations and misconceptions, turning what should be simple into a puzzle we struggle to solve. But happiness doesn't have to be elusive. It isn't waiting on the other side of an achievement or a perfectly planned life. It's already here, waiting to be uncovered in the choices we make, the relationships we nurture, and the moments we choose to embrace.

The idea for this book didn't come from abstract theories or lofty ideals. It grew from personal experience and a genuine curiosity about what makes people truly happy. Over the years, I've seen how subtle shifts in mindset, habits, and connections can transform lives—not in flashy or dramatic ways, but in ways that feel natural, meaningful, and sustainable.

This book is an invitation to step back from the noise and rediscover what happiness means for you—no grand gestures, no complicated formulas, just simple, practical steps that fit into the life you're already living. Life surrounds you, as you are reading this book right now.

This book is for anyone who has ever paused and asked themselves, "Am I truly happy?" Whether you're a young professional juggling career pressures and personal responsibilities, a parent navigating the beautiful chaos of raising a family, or someone simply seeking clarity amidst life's noise—this book is for you.

If you've felt the weight of daily distractions, the race to meet expectations, or the pull of comparison, you're not alone. This book was written with you in mind: someone who is ready to pause, reflect, and make meaningful changes that can bring clarity and fulfillment. It doesn't demand perfection or dramatic overhauls. It asks for curiosity, a willingness to try, and the courage to reflect.

Happiness isn't one-size-fits-all. What makes one person's heart sing might barely register for another. Yet, when you peel back the layers, certain truths begin to emerge. Happiness has roots, and those roots often lie in the simple, overlooked moments of our lives. It's the quiet pride in doing something meaningful. It's the warmth of a conversation that lingers in your heart long after it's over.

This book invites you to explore those roots—not with the pressure of finding perfect answers but with curiosity and openness. It's a chance to rediscover the joy of self-reflection and to embrace what feels right for you. Sometimes that means letting go of what no longer serves you, whether it's clutter or outdated expectations. Other times, it means noticing the relationships that bring light into your life or rethinking how you respond to everyday frustrations.

Happiness grows quietly in the background as you realign your habits, relationships, and mindset with what truly matters. This book guides you to those spaces, offering tools to cultivate joy and meaning in the life you already live.

Happiness, as you'll discover through these pages, isn't achieved by doing more but by focusing on what truly matters. As you move through the chapters, you'll learn to define happiness for yourself—not as something shaped by external pressures, but as a reflection of your own priorities.

Beware though—this isn't a passive read!

It's a hands-on guide filled with relatable stories and simple strategies you can start using immediately. Each chapter is an opportunity to reflect, to try something new, and to discover what makes your life feel lighter, calmer, and more connected.

At its core, this book reminds you of something powerful: happiness isn't a far-off goal or an item to tick off your to-do list. It's already within your reach, waiting for the choices you make, the connections you nurture, and the moments you pause to take in. Each little step brings you closer to a version of happiness that's entirely your own.

Happiness begins with you. It's in the choices you make, the moments you allow yourself to pause, and the connections you choose to nurture. It's not something to chase or fix—it's something you're already capable of finding right here, in the life you're living today.

This book isn't here to tell you what to do. It's here to remind you of what you already know deep down—that you have everything you need to create the happiness you deserve. So start where you are. Pay attention to what feels good, let go of what weighs you down, and trust yourself to take the next step, and turn the page.

Why wait? Happiness isn't something hidden in the future or waiting somewhere else—it's here, right now, in the moments you already hold.

Choose to embrace it, and when someone asks, "How did you find happiness?" simply say, "I created it myself."

Let's discover it together.

Chapter 1

CTRL + ALT + DEL

When was the last time you felt really happy?

Not just a quick smile for a photo or the automatic "I'm fine" you say when someone asks how you're doing, but a kind of happiness that feels real and sticks with you.

Think about it for a moment. Was it a few weeks ago? Months? Maybe even longer? Can you remember what it felt like to wake up and feel light, as if the day ahead wasn't already pressing down on you? When mornings weren't consumed by the mental checklist of everything you needed to do, but instead felt like a fresh start? Or what it was like to sit quietly with your thoughts, not overwhelmed by worry or stress, but at peace, letting your mind wander to happy places? Those moments may feel distant now, but think back—there was a time when you didn't carry so much weight.

Happiness like that doesn't happen by itself. It's not something you feel from crossing things off a to-do list, chasing validation, or simply rushing through your day. It's a feeling that comes when things feel natural and right like it's really yours. So, take a moment to truly reflect: when was the last time you felt that way?

Most days, life doesn't leave much space for that kind of joy. Your alarm rings before the sun is even up, and the first thing you see is your phone lighting up with notifications. Before you've even gotten out of bed, your mind is already racing—emails to check, deadlines to meet, errands to run, parents and kids to look after. By the time you take your first sip of coffee or chai, it feels like you're already behind. Yet again, you catch yourself 'running late', rushing through your morning routine—or skipping it entirely—as the clock ticks faster than you'd like. The day feels like it's already spiraling, pulling you along with no chance to catch up.

As the day moves on, the pressure builds. Your thoughts feel like they're all over the place, your shoulders are tense, and even the smallest sounds—a text notification, the hum of traffic, the chatter of people around you—feel like too much. Maybe your manager just handed you an extra task with an impossible deadline, or your kid casually mentioned they have a project due tomorrow. Then, at the worst possible moment, when you're already stretched thin, you're staring at your computer, and it freezes. The cursor doesn't move. The program won't close. The spinning wheel just sits there, and you feel stuck.

At that moment, as infinite and endless as it may seem, there's only one thing you can do:

Press "Ctrl + Alt + Del."

With one swift motion, the screen flickers, the chaos dissolves, and everything resets. The unresponsive programs vanish, the system breathes again, and you're left with a blank slate. It's as if, in that single action, you've reclaimed control over the chaos. The heaviness lifts, replaced by a sense of clarity and calm. You've started fresh, and for the first time in hours, it feels like things might be okay. Suddenly, the screen clears, the clutter is gone, and the system resets. Everything feels lighter, and easier, like you've been given a fresh start.

What if you could do that with your life? What if you could pause everything, take a moment to figure out what's working, and let go of the things that aren't? What if those three keys weren't just for computers but a way to reset your mind, clear the mental clutter, and make room for happiness that's already waiting for you?

"Ctrl + Alt + Del" is more than a shortcut for fixing frozen screens. For me, this keyboard shortcut became a way to reset my mindset and take control of my happiness. Each key holds a lesson—a step toward clarity, balance, and growth that can help you find your own fresh start. Here's how it works:

Ctrl: Pause

Sometimes, the best thing you can do is stop. In the middle of a busy day, when everything feels like it's spinning out of control, take a moment to breathe and reflect. Imagine hitting "Ctrl" in your own life to interrupt the chaos. It could be as simple as sitting down with a cup of tea, stepping outside for fresh air, or closing your eyes for a few quiet minutes. Pausing doesn't mean giving up; it means giving yourself the space to think clearly and decide what really matters.

I remember a moment in my own life when pausing made all the difference. It was during a week where every task felt urgent and every deadline loomed. Instead of pushing through, I stepped away for fifteen minutes and went for a walk. That small act of hitting "Ctrl" helped me regain perspective, and when I returned, I could tackle my work with renewed focus.

Alt: Explore

Once you've paused, it's time to look at things from a different angle. What's not working? What alternatives could you try? Often, we get stuck because we're too focused on one way of doing things. Exploring doesn't mean abandoning your goals; it means finding new paths to reach them. If a task is overwhelming, could you break it into smaller steps? If a situation feels unfixable, could you ask for help or rethink your approach?

Instead of struggling to finish a project that feels impossible, what if you asked a coworker for their perspective? Sometimes, a fresh pair of eyes can help you see solutions you've missed. Exploring alternatives is never about admitting defeat; it's about being flexible and creative in how you move forward.

Delete: Let Go

Let's face it: In life, not everything is worth holding onto. Some tasks, relationships, or habits weigh us down more than they lift us up. Hitting "Del" is about letting go of what no longer serves you. This doesn't have to be dramatic. It could be as simple as saying no to an unnecessary obligation, unfollowing accounts that drain your energy, or rethinking a routine that doesn't align with your values.

Sometimes, clearing space is the only way to make room for something better.

Sometimes, life demands a reset.

I was reminded of this when I heard the lyrics from Billy Talent's song *Perfect World*: "Control-Alt-Deleted… Reset my memory!"

That line stuck with me because it perfectly captured what so many of us need—a way to let go of bad memories, toxic patterns, or lingering negativity. Of course, we can't erase the past, but we can choose how much power it holds over us. Resetting doesn't mean forgetting; it means deciding what's worth carrying forward and what's not. And giving yourself permission to let go and move on, unburdened by the weight of yesterday. Imagine what your life could feel like if you could press "Reset" on the things that hold you back.

So, what in your life needs a reset? Take a moment to think about it. Is there something you need to pause and reflect on? A situation that could benefit from a new perspective? Or something you've been holding onto that it's finally time to let go of?

"Ctrl + Alt + Del" isn't just for computers. It's a tool you can use anytime to reset, refocus, and reclaim the happiness that's already within reach.

Insights from Human Behavior

I've always been fascinated by the way people carry themselves in public spaces. Sometimes, I like to sit in a park or a busy café and simply observe. One afternoon, I was at a park under the shade of a tree, watching life unfold around me. A woman was laughing with her child as she handed him an ice cream cone. Her smile radiated pure joy as he tried to manage the melting treat. Just a few benches away, a man sat slumped over, his head in his hands, looking completely weighed down by something unseen. The contrast was striking—how could two people, sharing the same sunny afternoon, experience it so differently?

That moment stayed with me. What makes one person carry lightness while another seems burdened by invisible weight? As I've observed more people over time, some patterns have stood out. Happier people don't deny life's challenges, but they don't let those challenges consume them either. They seem to have a way of embracing positivity while staying grounded in reality.

Another thing I've noticed is curiosity. Happier people are often curious about the world around them. Whether it's learning something new, exploring a hobby, or simply being open to fresh perspectives, their curiosity keeps them engaged and connected. They don't shy away from challenges; instead, they lean into discovery, and that brings a quiet sense of fulfillment.

Authenticity also plays a big role. Happier people tend to be themselves, wherever they are. They don't put on masks or try to be someone they're not. They're comfortable in their own skin, and that authenticity seems to create a kind of peace that carries them through life's ups and downs.

Science backs this up too. Studies show that curiosity improves mental health, boosts memory, and enhances problem-solving skills. One study from the *Journal of Personality* even found that curiosity makes people more emotionally resilient and better equipped to handle stress. When you're curious, your brain stays engaged and your emotions feel more balanced.

So, what can you learn by observing the world around you—and yourself? Start by noticing the moments that bring lightness to your day. Is it the aroma of freshly brewed chai shared with your family in the morning? The cheerful ring of the doorbell when a neighbor drops by for a quick chat? Or perhaps the sound of children playing cricket in the street, their laughter carrying the carefree joy we often long for? At the same time, pay attention to what feels heavy. Is it the pressure of juggling work deadlines and family commitments? Or the constant hum of comparisons scrolling through your social media feed? Identifying these moments can help you find clarity and focus on what truly matters.

Curiosity isn't tied to judgment. It means asking questions, exploring new possibilities, and noticing small changes that make life feel lighter. When you remain curious, you create space for growth—and in that space, happiness finds room to flourish!

Findings from Behavioral Science

Have you ever wondered how many emotions humans actually experience? Some researchers say there are 24, others argue for 27, and Psychologist Robert Plutchik believed that there may be as many as 34000 unique emotions humans can experience but he then simplified by identifying eight emotions and created a model known as "Wheel of Emotions". While the exact number is up for debate, most experts agree on six core emotions: happiness, anger, fear, sadness, disgust, and surprise. Out of these, happiness stands apart as the emotion we actively seek—the one we hope to hold onto for as long as possible.

So, what shapes happiness?

Research shows there are three key factors: genetics, environment, and choices. Genetics may set the baseline—some of us are naturally predisposed to be more optimistic than others. Environment plays a significant role too—the relationships we nurture, the spaces we inhabit, and the experiences we go through - all contribute to how happy we feel.

Yet, the most important factor is the one you have control over: your choices. Every day, the decisions you make determine how much space you allow for happiness in your life.

But, how often do we search for happiness in places that don't truly satisfy us?

Promotions, possessions, people, or recognition might feel rewarding in the moment, but that joy often fades quickly, leaving us chasing the next thing. It's easy to get caught in this cycle, isn't it? A pattern where happiness feels just out of reach, like it's always tied to what's next, instead of what's already here. It's like chasing a mirage—the closer you think you are, the further it moves away.

Here's where the "Ctrl + Alt + Del" metaphor can help us reset. When we pause to question what truly makes us happy, we often find that external validation isn't the answer. Instead, exploring what feels meaningful and letting go of unrealistic expectations can create space for genuine joy.

- **Ctrl:** Pause and question the pressures that drive you. Are you striving for something because it genuinely fulfills you, or because you think it should?

- **Alt:** Explore what truly brings satisfaction. Is it the material achievement, or the memories and connections that come with it?

- **Del:** Let go of the need for external validation. The opinions of others or societal expectations don't define your worth.

This realization becomes even clearer when you look at the people around you.

Over the years, I've noticed certain traits that happy people share. They're deeply self-aware, understanding their strengths and weaknesses without judgment. They practice gratitude, finding reasons to appreciate the small and big moments in life. They have a sense of humor, which helps them navigate challenges with ease. And most importantly, they forgive—both themselves and others—refusing to carry the weight of resentment that most of us so ungrudgingly hold on to without even realizing it.

I've met people who embody these principles. There's the friend who, after years of chasing titles and pay raises, realized her happiest moments came from teaching her daughter to bake—messy counters and all. Or the colleague who decided to leave the corporate hustle to start a small gardening business, trading stress for fulfillment. What they shared was self-awareness, gratitude, and the ability to forgive—themselves and others.

Science supports these traits. Studies show that self-awareness helps us align our actions with our values. Gratitude rewires the brain to focus on the positives. Humor reduces stress, and forgiveness releases the weight of resentment. And I'll let you in on a secret—these aren't impossible ideals; they're small, practical steps you can start today.

What intentional choices can you make right now? Maybe it's celebrating a small win—like finishing a task or savoring a meal you love. Perhaps it's exploring a hobby that brings you joy or reaching out to someone whose laughter always lightens your mood. Happiness doesn't rely on grand gestures; it's built from the little moments you choose to create and share each day.

The Value of Shared Joy

Have you ever noticed how happiness feels bigger when it's shared?

Think of a time you told a friend good news and saw their face light up with excitement. Or when you celebrated a small win with your family, and their joy made the moment even sweeter. Happiness has a way of multiplying when we let others in.

As Albert Schweitzer once said, "Happiness is the only thing that multiplies when you share it."

But sharing happiness doesn't have to be loud or dramatic. In fact, the most meaningful moments often come quietly. It could be as simple as bringing home someone's favorite snack, sending a kind message, or making time to listen to someone who needs it. These small gestures ripple outward, creating connections that not only lift others but also deepen your own sense of joy.

I've seen this in my own life. For years, I made it a habit to celebrate every milestone, no matter how small. When I got a promotion at work, I would treat myself to a new book or a special meal. But I also made it a point to share those moments with the people closest to me—my family, my friends, even colleagues who supported me along the way. There's something powerful about letting others be part of your joy. It's more than marking an achievement—it's weaving connections that make life feel rich and meaningful.

This isn't only true for big milestones. Even in the every day, sharing happiness can transform simple moments into cherished ones. I remember meeting a tea vendor on a solo bike trip. It was a small tea shop with six chairs and some basic snacks, but when I arrived, there was no one to attend to customers. After about five minutes, a smiling man arrived with three or four friends. One of them was the tea vendor. Before starting, he cleaned everything and handed me a chocolate. I smiled and said, "No thank you, I just need tea." One of his friends chimed in, "Take it, sir, it's a special day today." The vendor had bought a bicycle for his child, and his joy was infectious. While we chatted over tea, they shared that their village was small, and everyone treated each other like family. Every celebration, big or small, involved the entire community. I later learned that their village had even won an award for being the 'Happiest Village.' That memory stayed with me as I returned to the chaos of city life. It reminded me how sharing happiness strengthens bonds and spreads joy exponentially. Personally, I've started sharing my joys more deliberately with the people around me—at work, at home, and even with acquaintances. It's a practice that continues to enrich my life in unexpected ways.

Sharing doesn't have to be limited to celebrations, either. Sometimes, it's as simple as being present for someone else. A genuine "How are you doing?" can mean the world to someone who feels unseen. And when we share moments of joy, no matter how small, we create a ripple effect that carries far beyond ourselves.

So, here's a thought: what joys can you share today? Maybe it's as simple as calling a friend to tell them something that made you smile, or surprising a family member with their favorite dessert. Or maybe it's celebrating your own progress in a way that invites others to join in.

Happiness doesn't grow in isolation. The more you share it, the more it expands—not just for you, but for everyone it touches. Start small, and watch how those ripples turn into waves. Because in the end, happiness isn't something we keep; it's something we pass on.

Remember, happiness is just a choice away if you're brave and willing enough to choose it for yourself.

Chapter 2

HOW I CAN BE HAPPY?

After everything we explored in the last chapter, you might be wondering: "This all sounds great, but how can I be happy?"

Let's be honest—this is a question we've all asked ourselves at some point, maybe more often than you'd like to admit. It's not a new one either. Philosophers, thinkers, writers, and even teenagers on social media have struggled with it. And just like the variety of people asking, the answers have been equally diverse. Maybe you've even found yourself googling it at 2 a.m., scrolling through articles that promise to reveal the secret formula.

It's tempting to hope that happiness is simple—a button to press, a magic checklist to follow, or a solution someone else has already figured out for us. But here's the truth: happiness isn't prepackaged. There's no one-size-fits-all answer. What I can promise, though, is this: happiness isn't as complicated as we often make it. It's something you create, bit by bit, through small, intentional choices.

And where does it begin? By figuring out what works for you—understanding yourself in a way that goes beyond surface-level likes and dislikes. What energizes you? What brings you peace? What truly makes you feel alive? You might have to be your own test subject, experimenting and learning as you go. But isn't that the beauty of it? Discovering your own formula for joy?

We've talked about resetting, refocusing, and reclaiming your happiness. Now comes the real challenge: how do you actually do it? How do you move from feeling stuck to building a life that feels lighter and more fulfilling?

It all begins with one thing: practicing happiness. Not chasing it, not hoping for it, but practicing it—one step, one choice at a time. Let's start, right here, right now.

Self Experimentation

Have you ever second-guessed a decision, only to wish you'd paused to reflect before acting? It's a familiar feeling—realizing in hindsight that things could've been different if you'd listened to your inner voice. That's where self-awareness comes in, but let's be honest: tuning into yourself isn't always easy.

It's far simpler to blame the weather, traffic, or even other people for a bad day. We've all done it. But how often do we stop and look inward? How often do we ask ourselves: What role did I play in how I'm feeling? What choices led me here? Understanding yourself isn't about finding faults; it's about gaining clarity. And that's where self-experimentation can be a game-changer.

Self-experimentation is exactly what it sounds like: using yourself as a test subject to figure out what truly works for your happiness. You become the operator, designer, and evaluator of your own life experiments. It's a process of trying, observing, and adjusting until you discover what brings you joy, peace, and fulfillment.

When I first started experimenting with my own happiness, I realized how challenging it was to see myself clearly. It's one thing to offer advice to a friend, but turning that leans inward is another story entirely. Imagine giving yourself the same feedback you'd offer someone else. It's uncomfortable, but it's transformative. Over time, I learned to step back and view my actions and habits objectively—almost as if I were studying someone else.

One tool that helped me tremendously was the Johari Window.

It's a simple framework that divides self-awareness into four quadrants:

1. What you know about yourself and share with others (open).
2. What others see but you don't (blind).
3. What you keep hidden from others (hidden).
4. What neither you nor others know yet (unknown).

Working through these quadrants taught me to uncover hidden truths and close the gaps in my self-awareness. I started by listing out what I knew about myself—the strengths I leaned on and the habits I often ignored. For the "blind" quadrant, I asked trusted friends and colleagues for honest feedback, and their insights opened my eyes to tendencies I hadn't noticed, like how I sometimes overcommit to projects.

For the "hidden" quadrant, I reflected on what I kept private and why—it was a chance to explore how vulnerability might create deeper connections. The "unknown" quadrant required patience; I kept a journal, noting moments that surprised me, whether good or bad and over time, patterns emerged. This structured approach gave me clarity and helped me understand myself in ways I never had before.

For example, I realized that I often said yes to too many projects or tasks, not recognizing how overwhelmed I was until it hit me all at once. I remember this one time, I had agreed to help organize a work event, volunteer for a community project, and prepare for a family gathering all in the same week. By midweek, I was juggling so many responsibilities that I barely had time to eat properly, let alone reflect on how I was feeling. When I finally paused to take stock, I could see how I had set myself up for burnout by not setting boundaries.

That moment of clarity became a turning point—it helped me understand the importance of saying no when needed and focusing on commitments that aligned with my values and capacity. By observing this pattern, I could start saying no to unnecessary commitments and focus on what truly mattered.

Of course, self-experimentation isn't always easy. Seeing yourself from the outside can feel unnatural at first. But starting small makes it manageable. At the end of each day, I began asking myself two simple questions: What worked well today? And what didn't? By reflecting without judgment, I started to notice patterns—moments that brought me joy and moments that didn't.

I found that starting my mornings with a few quiet minutes—whether sipping tea or simply sitting in silence—made my entire day feel more balanced. On the flip side, I noticed that mindlessly scrolling through my phone before bed left me feeling restless and disconnected. These small observations became the foundation for bigger changes.

So, where can you start?

Think of one habit or routine in your life that feels heavy or unproductive. Experiment with small adjustments and observe how they make you feel. Maybe it's swapping ten minutes of screen time for journaling, or saying no to one obligation so you can say yes to something you love. The goal isn't perfection—it's progress. Self-experimentation lays the foundation for understanding what truly brings happiness. Once you uncover what lights you up, the next step is incorporating those passions into your daily life.

Pursuing Passions Daily

What brings you joy? Not fleeting happiness, but the kind of joy that makes you feel alive and grounded. For me, it's music. I've been playing the guitar and keyboard for over 20 years, but there was a time when work and responsibilities pushed it to the sidelines. Weeks turned into months, and before I knew it, I couldn't remember the last time I'd picked up my guitar. Life felt like it was missing something, but I couldn't quite put my finger on it.

Then, one day, I decided to carve out just 15 minutes for music. It wasn't much, but it was enough to reconnect with something that had always brought me joy. The first time I played again, I felt a spark—a reminder of what it felt like to do something purely for myself. Those 15 minutes became my daily ritual, and over time, they transformed my mindset. The stress of the day felt lighter, and my evenings ended on a happier note.

Making time for your passions isn't always easy, especially when life feels overwhelming. But you'll discover that joy doesn't simply happen—you have to create space for it. That's where time management becomes your best friend.

I learned this the hard way. I've always loved reading, playing cricket, and watching documentaries, but trying to squeeze everything into one day was impossible. The clock only has 24 hours, after all. So, I started planning my time more intentionally. I set aside 30 minutes for reading, 1 hour for cricket, and shorter blocks for music or movies. It wasn't about doing everything every day; it was about finding balance.

One of the most important lessons I learned was how to say no. For years, I said yes to every request and invitation, often at the expense of my own happiness. But saying yes to everything meant saying no to myself. Learning to decline unnecessary obligations gave me the freedom to prioritize what truly mattered. And once I did, my days began to feel fuller, not busier.

At first, creating a routine for my hobbies felt like an effort, but over time, it became second nature. Playing the guitar, reading, or heading out for a game of cricket became as automatic as brushing my teeth—a part of my life I couldn't imagine skipping. These routines weren't just activities; they became moments of joy woven into my day.

So, what's your passion? Maybe it's painting, gardening, dancing, or even experimenting in the kitchen. Whatever it is, start small. Set aside 10 or 15 minutes a day to do something you love. It doesn't have to be perfect or productive—it just has to make you happy. Over time, those moments of joy will add up, creating a foundation of happiness that carries you through even the busiest days.

Imagine setting aside time to do something that makes you smile—every single day. The effects ripple outward. You'll notice your mood improving, your stress levels dropping, and even your relationships feeling more harmonious. It's not magic; it's the result of carving out space for what truly matters.

When you pursue what lights you up, even in small doses, it reminds you that life isn't all work and obligation. It's also connection, laughter, and the quiet satisfaction of doing something just for you.

Now, think about this: what's one thing you've always loved but haven't made time for lately? Maybe it's been months since you dusted off your sketchbook or years since you stepped onto a dance floor. Start with 10 minutes a day. Let it be a gift you give yourself—a moment to breathe, smile, and reconnect with the parts of you that might have been tucked away.

Pursuing passions brings joy, but to truly sustain that happiness, we need to stay mindful of our progress and emotions. That's where journaling comes in.

Journaling and Reflection

Have you ever ended a day feeling drained but couldn't quite pinpoint why? Journaling can help uncover the patterns behind those emotions. For me, it started as a simple habit. At the end of each day, I'd sit down with a notebook and create three columns: what worked, what didn't, and what brought me happiness. The goal wasn't to judge or fix everything overnight; it was to observe and learn.

One evening, I noticed a recurring pattern in my entries. On days when I skipped my guitar practice, I often felt restless and irritable. Conversely, even a quick five-minute session made me feel accomplished and at ease. That realization encouraged me to prioritize music, even on busy days. Another discovery came from a small but powerful ritual: smiling in the mirror each morning. It felt silly at first, but it set a positive tone for the day ahead. Over time, these little habits added up, creating a noticeable shift in my mood and energy.

A friend of mine had a similar approach but took it a step further. He used a five-column journaling method that included what went well, what didn't, what he was grateful for, what he'd like to improve, and one small action for the next day. His goal wasn't perfection but progress. By focusing on gratitude and solutions rather than dwelling on problems, he found himself worrying less and smiling more.

One of the most striking things he shared with me was how he stopped judging himself and others. Instead of fixating on mistakes, he wrote down lessons learned and steps to avoid repeating them. This shift in perspective made a huge difference in his overall happiness.

If you're new to journaling, start simple. At the end of your day, ask yourself three questions: What made you smile today? What felt heavy? What's one thing you can try tomorrow to make it better? Write your answers without overthinking. The act of putting thoughts on paper creates clarity and helps you track emotional progress over time.

Rereading your entries can be just as enlightening. It's a chance to see how far you've come and identify the small changes that have made a big impact. For example, you might notice that prioritizing a morning walk consistently boosts your mood or that spending less time on social media leaves you feeling lighter. These insights are invaluable for shaping a life that feels more aligned with what truly makes you happy.

Journaling isn't about writing perfect prose or recording every detail of your day. It's a tool for reflection, growth, and mindfulness. Each entry is a step toward understanding yourself better and creating space for joy. The key is to approach it with curiosity and kindness—not as a chore, but as a gift you give yourself!

Tracking your emotions and progress helps you stay connected to what matters most. The more you reflect, the easier it becomes to notice patterns that guide you toward a fulfilling life. This awareness not only shows you what makes you happy but also helps you build the mindset and habits to stay that way.

Developing Core Happiness Traits

On a long drive back from my hometown, my car broke down near the border of a small village. It was mid-afternoon, the sun casting long shadows as the hours dragged on, and help seemed like a distant hope. An elderly lady at a nearby shop noticed our predicament and welcomed us with tea and snacks, offering a shaded spot to rest while we waited. She treated us like family, saying, "You are like my son and daughter-in-law. If I can help, I will." Her kindness left an impression that stayed with me long after. In that moment, I learned something that has stuck with me ever since: happiness isn't merely what we feel—it's what we give and receive through genuine, heartfelt gestures.

That experience was a reminder that the core of happiness often lies in traits like gratitude, kindness, and resilience. Happier people don't avoid challenges altogether. Instead, they cultivate attitudes that bring lightness, even when life feels heavy.

- **Gratitude:** Gratitude is the ability to appreciate what you have, no matter how small it may seem. It's not about ignoring difficulties but recognizing the good that exists alongside them. After the car incident, I found myself more grateful for the small acts of kindness I encountered daily—a smile from a stranger, an encouraging word from a friend, or the simple joy of a clear sky. Gratitude shifts your focus from what's lacking to what's present, creating a sense of abundance.

- **Kindness:** Kindness, like gratitude, creates ripples that extend beyond the moment. The elderly lady's generosity reminded me that helping others often feels as rewarding as receiving help. Acts of kindness don't have to be grand. They can be as simple as holding the door for someone, offering a listening ear, or sharing a laugh with a coworker. These moments create connections and foster a sense of belonging that enriches both the giver and the receiver.

- **Resilience:** Resilience is the ability to face setbacks without losing hope. During that breakdown, I could have focused on the inconvenience or spiraled into frustration. Instead, I chose to accept the situation and trust that things would work out. Later, I learned that my delay had saved me from hours of traffic ahead. Sometimes, resilience means surrendering to the moment, finding silver linings, and working toward a solution rather than dwelling on the problem.

These traits aren't innate; they're habits you can nurture. Start small. Send a thank-you message to someone who's helped you recently. Offer a kind gesture to a neighbor or colleague. The next time something doesn't go as planned, pause and ask yourself, "What can I learn from this?"

Over time, these small actions add up, shaping a mindset that embraces gratitude, kindness, and resilience. They help you focus on what you can control and let go of what you can't, creating space for happiness to grow.

Happiness isn't chasing perfection. It's built on the foundation of self-discovery, daily joys, mindful reflection, and core traits that align with your values. The more you practice, the more these habits will become second nature, guiding you toward a truly fulfilling life. Start small, stay consistent, and watch happiness grow—one intentional moment at a time.

Chapter 3

DON'T BE MATERIALISTIC

The road stretched endlessly ahead, the sky a restless gray.

You remember the tea vendor from my solo bike trip—the one who greeted me with his warm smile and shared simple, heartfelt kindness? After I left his cheerful stall and continued on my journey, the air seemed heavier, the world quieter. The warmth of his hospitality lingered in my thoughts as I rode on, but soon the sky darkened, and a sudden downpour caught me off guard.

I pulled over under a sprawling tree by the side of the road, hoping the branches would provide some shelter. The raindrops hammered against the leaves in a steady rhythm, soaking through my jacket. As I waited, a car approached and slowed to a stop nearby. The window rolled down, and inside was an elderly couple with kind, inviting faces.

"You shouldn't wait out here in the rain," the man said, his voice warm and steady. "Come to our house. It's nearby. Have some tea while the storm passes."

Their invitation was warm, genuine—the kind you don't overthink. I nodded, grateful, and followed their car to their home. It was a modest yet beautiful place, with a neatly tended garden bursting with marigolds and a swing that creaked gently in the wind. The aunt welcomed me with a steaming cup of coffee and a plate of onion pakodas—crispy, golden, and somehow exactly what I needed. As we sat in their cozy living room, I felt a calmness settle over me. The storm outside seemed miles away.

The uncle joined us, his eyes twinkling with the kind of contentment that feels rare these days. We began to chat, and I couldn't resist asking, "Uncle, you seem so relaxed and happy. What's your secret?"

He smiled and leaned forward, his voice steady and thoughtful. "Two things," he said.

"First, I've earned enough to fulfill my needs. Second, I don't chase what I don't need." He paused, letting the words sink in. "Being materialistic is a curse for your happiness."

That line stuck with me.

It wasn't the first time I'd heard someone speak against materialism, but the simplicity of his truth—spoken in a home filled with warmth rather than excess—hit differently. As he explained further, I realized how closely his words echoed my own reflections from the journey so far—that true happiness often slips away when we pin it on material things.

A bigger car, a newer phone, a flashier wardrobe—we tell ourselves these will make us happy. And don't get me wrong- they do, but only for a fleeting moment. But before long, the thrill fades, and we're left wanting more.

Think about it. Maybe you recently bought a gadget you'd been eyeing, a piece of furniture that seemed perfect for your home, or a pair of shoes that caught your attention. For a while, you felt that surge of satisfaction, but then it faded—perhaps faster than you expected. The initial excitement wears off, leaving you wondering if it was really worth it.? That initial rush, psychologists say, is called the "honeymoon phase" of material satisfaction. But like a fleeting romance, it doesn't last.

The uncle's words came alive as I thought about my own life. How many times had I been swept up in the excitement of a new purchase, only to feel its charm wear off once the novelty faded? The problem isn't the things themselves—it's the expectation we place on them to fill a deeper void.

We confuse momentary pleasure with lasting happiness.

The curse of materialism lies in its ability to create a never-ending cycle that not only drains your finances but also weighs heavily on your mental well-being and relationships. When we tie our happiness to things, we often lose sight of what truly matters. The constant yearning for the next upgrade or latest trend can lead to feelings of inadequacy and frustration, straining our connections with others as we prioritize possessions over meaningful moments.

It's a cycle that's easy to fall into but hard to escape, making it all the more important to recognize its impact on our lives. When the shine of one possession fades, we look for the next. A newer model, a better design, a fancier brand—we convince ourselves that this time, it will be different. But the truth is, possessions can't give us what we're really searching for.

Take a moment to think about your own relationship with possessions. Perhaps it's a new gadget you couldn't wait to unbox or a pair of shoes you've been eyeing for weeks. Did it bring a sense of lasting happiness, or was it more about the momentary excitement of owning something new? Reflecting on this can offer surprising insights into how possessions influence our sense of contentment.? Did it genuinely add lasting happiness to your life, or was it more about the thrill of acquiring it? Thinking about these questions might feel a bit uncomfortable, but it can be really eye-opening. It's not about feeling guilty—it's about building awareness.

As I sat with the uncle and aunt that day, sipping coffee and soaking in their simplicity, I understood something deep. Happiness isn't in the things we own. It's in the moments we share, the people we connect with, and the peace we find in appreciating what we already have. That day, as I sat with the uncle and aunt, I couldn't help but see how their lives reflected this wisdom. Their home wasn't filled with excess, but it overflowed with contentment, warmth, and kindness—a reminder that true richness comes from what we give and how we choose to live.

And sometimes, it's in the gift of a warm cup of coffee on a rainy day.

The Stress of Materialism

Have you ever opened your closet, brimming with clothes you haven't wore in years, or cricket gear that gathers dust in the corner? Yet, somehow, it still feels like something is missing.

This is the paradox of materialism: the more we accumulate, the more it demands from us. Every item comes with its own weight, not just in physical space but in mental load. Think of the last time you bought something new—a stylish jacket, an intricate piece of decor, or perhaps even a kitchen appliance. For a while, it felt exciting, didn't it? But how long did that feeling last?

The problem with possessions is that they often create more stress than joy. The more you own, the more you have to maintain. A closet filled with clothes you barely wear, gadgets that need constant updates, or even decorative items that collect dust—all these things demand your time and attention. Decision fatigue sets in, like standing in front of an overflowing closet and struggling to pick the right outfit, even though you only ever reach for your favorite few.

But really, who can blame us? There's so much pressure to keep up. Social media is full of pictures of people's new cars, designer bags, and the latest phones—it's hard not to get caught up! It's easy to feel like you're falling behind, even if you were perfectly content moments before. This endless comparison not only drains your wallet but also your mental peace. The joy of owning something new quickly turns into the anxiety of maintaining it, posting it, or the itch to upgrade.

I remember going to the mall once, planning to buy just a pair of jeans. Simple, right? But as I wandered through the aisles, all the bright displays and tempting offers got me. I walked out with not just jeans, but a shirt, a watch, and a bag I didn't even need. At first, it felt exciting, but by the time I got home, the thrill had completely worn off. None of those things made me as happy as I thought they would—they just added to the pile of stuff I barely used.

And don't even get me started on my shoe collection. Over the years, I somehow ended up with so many pairs—formal shoes, sneakers, sandals, you name it. But every morning, I'd reach for the same comfy pair, while the rest just sat there collecting dust. It made me wonder why I even bought so many in the first place. All that time spent picking, maintaining, or feeling guilty about neglecting them could've been put to better use.

Excess possessions don't just clutter our homes; they clutter our minds.

The more we focus on managing what we have, the less time and energy we have to enjoy life. It's a cycle that can leave us feeling empty, no matter how much we acquire. When we attach our happiness to objects, we give those objects power over us. And when they fail to deliver, as they inevitably do, we're left chasing the next thing, hoping it will finally fill the gap.

Take a moment to reflect.

What's in your home that you haven't used in months? Maybe it's wedding gifts still in their original packaging, festival decorations stored away year-round, or clothes from a shopping spree that never saw the light of day. Could letting go of those items create space—not only in your home but also in your mind—for what truly matters? Imagine opening a closet or stepping into a room and seeing only what you love and use. The simplicity would feel freeing, wouldn't it?

The uncle's wisdom echoed in my mind as I thought about this. His home wasn't filled with things; it was filled with peace—a peace that came from embracing simplicity and aligning his life with the traditional Indian philosophy of valuing what truly matters. It reminded me of Gandhian principles, where detachment from excess and focus on needs over wants are seen as ways to contentment and harmony. That peace came from understanding the difference between needs and wants and choosing to value the moments and connections that truly matter.

It's a lesson that stays with me and one that I hope you'll carry forward, too.

Shifting to Intrinsic Values

Revisiting that conversation with the uncle, one question he asked me still resonates: "Do I need this, or do I want it?" Such a straightforward question, yet it held a lifetime of wisdom. He explained how this question shaped his decisions, whether it was a practical purchase like an appliance or the allure of upgrading his car. "Is it for my use," he asked, "or am I buying it to impress others?"

His perspective made me rethink my own habits. He used cars as an example, comparing the pull of a top-of-the-line model with features that often go unused to owning a simple car that meets all your needs. "The car isn't the journey," he said. "What matters is who you're traveling with and the memories you create along the way." That idea stuck with me. How often do we chase the newest gadgets, not because we need them, but because they're shiny, new, and promise a better life? Yet, that excitement fades quickly, leaving us wanting more.

I reflected on a smartphone I bought a few years ago. I was drawn to its sleek design and advanced features, many of which I hardly used. At the time, I convinced myself it would improve my productivity. But within months, a newer model was released, and the cycle of wanting began again. That phone didn't bring lasting happiness. Instead, it became a symbol of how easily I'd been caught up in consumerism.

Changing this mindset wasn't easy, but it was worth it. I started asking myself the uncle's questions before making decisions: Why do I want this? Will it genuinely add value to my life, or is it just another distraction? These questions became a filter, helping me focus on what truly mattered. Mindful consumption isn't about depriving yourself; it's about making choices that align with your values and purpose.

Over time, I realized that joy doesn't come from what we own but from the experiences we create. Taking a road trip in a modest car or sharing a home-cooked meal with friends felt infinitely more fulfilling when I wasn't distracted by material desires. Happiness found its way into the quiet moments—a heartfelt conversation, a peaceful walk, or completing a meaningful task.

So, before your next purchase, pause and ask yourself: "Why do I want this? How will it serve my life?" This simple act of questioning can change how you view your choices, shifting your focus to what genuinely aligns with your happiness.

As I reflected further, I kept returning to the uncle's wisdom. His approach wasn't abstract; it was grounded in real-life simplicity and thoughtful living. By embracing this perspective, he had created a life of contentment and purpose. It's a lesson I've carried with me and one I hope will inspire you to think differently about what truly brings joy.

Moving away from material possessions doesn't mean giving up comfort or convenience. It means being thoughtful—choosing what genuinely serves your life and letting go of what doesn't. In doing so, you create space for the joys that can't be bought: meaningful connections, a sense of purpose, and the quiet assurance that you already have enough.

Retail Therapy, aka, Misplaced Happiness

Let's talk about retail therapy. We've all done it—no judgment here.

Retail therapy is something many of us turn to without a second thought. After all, it feels so simple—step into a store or scroll through an online site, hoping to buy something that might lift your spirits. It's the same pattern we've seen in materialism's allure throughout this chapter—a quick fix for something deeper, often rooted in the fleeting satisfaction of owning more. And for a moment, it works. That new jacket or gadget feels exciting, like a spark of joy in an otherwise stressful day. But how long does that feeling last? A few hours? A week? Before you know it, the jacket hangs unworn in your closet, and the gadget is gathering dust. The thrill fades, replaced by regret or indifference.

A friend of mine comes to mind when I think about this cycle. He's always upgrading his phone, chasing the latest model as soon as it's released. I remember him eagerly unboxing the latest device, his excitement palpable as he explored its features. For a few days, he was all smiles, showing it off and talking about its specs. But not long after, the novelty wore off. When a newer model was announced, his enthusiasm shifted—his current phone no longer seemed enough. He confessed that he often felt a fleeting sense of satisfaction, quickly replaced by the pressure to keep up with others, leaving him in a constant loop of want and dissatisfaction. He tells himself it's necessary—better features, faster performance. But within months, a new model comes out, and the excitement evaporates. He's left feeling unsatisfied, already looking for the next upgrade. It's not the phone he's chasing; it's a sense of worth, of keeping up with his peers. But that kind of happiness is fleeting—a momentary high that never lasts.

I've seen this play out in other ways, too. A close friend of mine faced this dilemma shortly after getting married. His wife, eager to match her colleagues' recent purchases, began insisting on buying a new car. One of her colleagues had purchased a shiny vehicle, and she didn't want to feel left behind. My friend, however, had been saving for a home—something they both had dreamed of. He tried reasoning with her, asking to delay the car purchase and focus on their long-term goal.

Despite his efforts, the pressure to keep up won out, and they bought the car. For a few months, it brought her joy—a sense of pride that she could show to her colleagues. But as the excitement faded, the financial strain became evident. Their lives fell out of balance as they struggled to align their priorities with reality. She had relied on others' choices for her happiness, leaving them both stuck in a cycle of dissatisfaction.

These examples aren't unique. They mirror the uncle's wisdom about distinguishing between needs and wants. When we link our happiness to possessions, we often fall into the trap of chasing validation through things, rather than finding contentment within ourselves. But here's the truth: when we chase material things for validation, the satisfaction is always temporary. We buy to impress, to compete, or to fill a void, but the joy never comes from the item itself. It comes from within, from a sense of purpose and connection that can't be bought.

So, what's the alternative?

Start by shifting your focus. Instead of chasing things, celebrate experiences. Instead of seeking validation through possessions, invest in relationships and personal growth. For example, think about the last time you shared a meal with loved ones or took a walk in the park. Those moments leave a deeper mark than any purchase ever could.

The next time you feel the urge to shop, pause and ask yourself: What emotion am I trying to fill? Are you reaching for something because you're feeling stressed, lonely, or bored? Instead of clicking "add to cart," consider calling a friend to share a laugh, stepping outside for fresh air, or revisiting an old hobby that brings you peace. Redirecting that momentary impulse can lead to something far more fulfilling.? Are you stressed? Bored? Feeling left out? Recognizing the emotion behind the impulse can help you redirect your energy toward something more meaningful. Call a friend, pick up a hobby, or simply take a moment to breathe. You might find that the urge to shop fades, replaced by a deeper sense of satisfaction.

Breaking free from materialism isn't about giving up on nice things. It's about embracing the uncle's wisdom—distinguishing between needs and wants—and making choices that align with your values. By focusing on what genuinely serves your life, you open the door to contentment that no possession can provide. When you let go of the need to compete or compare, you open the door to a life that's richer in ways money can't buy. By focusing on intrinsic values—like connection, creativity, and purpose—you'll discover a happiness that lasts.

As you turn the page, think about the uncle's wisdom and how it can transform your own life. Simplifying isn't just about less clutter—it's about more clarity. By letting go of excess, whether in your surroundings or your mind, you create space for the things that truly matter.

How? Let's find out in the next chapter!

Chapter 4

MINIMALISM IS THE KEY

"Minimalism is one of the greatest ways to maximize your happiness"

The sunlight streaming through the windows barely reached the floor. It was crowded with boxes stacked haphazardly, items spilling out—clothes, papers, bags, and odds and ends. It was the kind of mess that had slowly built over time, never feeling like a priority to address.

But one day, as I stared at the chaos, it struck me: this wasn't only a cluttered room. It was a reflection of how my mind felt—crowded, overwhelmed, and drained.

That realization marked the beginning of my journey toward minimalism. Minimalism wasn't an extreme change; it was a shift toward clarity and purpose. It was clearing the excess to make room for what truly mattered. The boxes weren't the problem; it was the constant mental tug-of-war they created—what to keep, what to toss, why I hadn't used half of it in years. It wasn't the physical mess that bothered me most; it was the distraction and stress it carried with it.

Lessons from the Pandemic

I still remember that call from the office in March 2020.

It was short and to the point: we were transitioning to work from home for two weeks. The message included a warning—if you were traveling, you would need to isolate for an extra week after returning. With that in mind, I packed lightly for what I thought would be a short visit to my hometown: a couple of sets of clothes, my laptop, and a few essentials. It didn't seem worth overpacking for a fortnight.

But within a week of arriving, the world changed. The word "lockdown" became part of our everyday vocabulary, and life as we knew it came to a standstill. Suddenly, the two-week trip stretched into months, and the light packing I had done turned into an unintentional exercise in minimalism. What could have felt like a limitation ended up being an eye-opener. The few items I had packed were enough—enough to live, enough to work, and, most importantly, enough to find happiness.

The pandemic disrupted lives in ways we had never experienced before. It brought stress, uncertainty, and even fear for our safety. But amidst the chaos, it also taught us valuable lessons. With fewer distractions, it became clear that life didn't need to be so complicated. Many people found joy in simple routines: home-cooked meals, connecting virtually with loved ones, and rediscovering hobbies that had been set aside in the rush of daily life.

I remember speaking with a friend during this time, someone who had always lived life as if it were a race. His philosophy had always been to spend, enjoy, and worry later. But the lockdown changed him. With no malls to visit and no fancy dinners to attend, he found himself saving money for the first time. He even started looking into investment plans—a far cry from his earlier mindset.

The shift wasn't just personal. Across society, priorities changed. A shopkeeper I knew mentioned that his bestsellers during the lockdown weren't flashy outfits or designer wear but simple items like pyjamas, daily wear, and comfortable clothing. People were no longer dressing to impress but dressing for themselves. Staying at home 24/7 made many realize how little they actually needed to be content.

Being confined to our homes forced us to confront our own spaces and thoughts. The saying "Jaan hai to jahan hai"—"If there's life, then there's everything"—resonated deeply. It became evident that health, family, and mental well-being were far more valuable than possessions or appearances. This period made us reevaluate what truly mattered: not the extravagant vacations we couldn't take but the simple joys of being safe, being together, and being alive.

For me, the time spent with family was priceless. I found joy in the smallest moments: eating meals with my parents, reading books that had been gathering dust, and indulging in hobbies I'd forgotten I loved. Life slowed down, but in that stillness, there was clarity. The pandemic showed us that less truly is enough—not only in terms of possessions but also in terms of mental clutter.

We didn't need grand plans or endless options to feel fulfilled. We needed purpose, connection, and gratitude.

Minimalism is often mistaken for deprivation, but the lockdown taught me that it's the opposite. It's not about giving things up; it's about holding onto what matters. It's about simplifying, not sacrificing. Less isn't merely manageable; it's liberating. It frees you from the constant pull of wants, allowing you to focus on the richness of what you already have.

The lockdown also revealed the importance of mental decluttering.

With nowhere to go and fewer distractions, we had to confront our thoughts. It became essential to filter out the noise and focus on what added value to our lives. Minimizing unnecessary worries—whether through meditation, journaling, or simply taking things one day at a time—became as important as minimizing possessions.

The lessons from that time are worth carrying forward.

Life can be simpler and more fulfilling when we prioritize essentials over excess, needs over wants. When we stop chasing what's unnecessary, we find space—both physical and mental—for what brings true happiness.

The pandemic didn't merely teach us to live with less; it showed us how to find joy in it. The question is: how can we bring that simplicity into our everyday lives?

Practical Steps to Simplify Life

If you took a walk through your home today, how many items would you find that were bought impulsively, to impress others, or as a quick fix for stress? Chances are, there would be more than a few. These aren't just things—they're the silent clutter that fills not only your spaces but also your mind, weighing you down in ways you might not even notice until the burden feels overwhelming.

Simplifying life begins with small, intentional steps. It's not about discarding everything; it's about reassessing what truly adds value. Start with one room or even a single drawer. Pick up each item and ask yourself, "Do I use this? Does it bring me joy? Would I miss it if it were gone?" These simple questions can transform how you view your belongings, helping you make decisions that create a sense of lightness—not only in your space but also in your mind.

This principle applies equally to your digital life. How many apps sit on your phone untouched for months? How many files clutter your desktop, making it hard to find what you actually need? Decluttering digitally can feel as liberating as clearing out a crowded closet. Delete the apps you don't use, organize your photos, and limit notifications to only what truly matters. A clean digital space leads to a clearer headspace, allowing you to focus on what's important.

Mindful spending is another crucial step. Real happiness doesn't come from accumulating more. As Hosea Ballou wisely said, "Real happiness is cheap enough, yet how dearly we pay for its counterfeit." Create a budget and track your expenses, no matter how small. The next time you feel the urge to shop, pause and ask yourself, "Am I buying this out of need or impulse? Will it genuinely add value to my life?" Often, replacing the habit of shopping therapy with meaningful activities—like exercising, reading, or spending time with loved ones—brings a deeper and more lasting satisfaction, free from buyer's remorse.

This mindset extends beyond your possessions. Simplifying your social life and commitments is equally important. How often do we say yes to obligations that don't match our priorities, out of guilt or habit? Learning to say no—politely but firmly—creates space for what truly aligns with your values. It's not about doing less; it's about doing what matters most.

Even your thoughts can benefit from a minimalist approach. Too often, our minds are crowded with worries, regrets, and endless to-do lists. Practices like journaling or meditation help sift through this mental clutter, allowing you to focus on what's essential and let go of the rest. A decluttered mind is calmer, more present, and better equipped to handle life's challenges.

When I began decluttering my wardrobe, it wasn't just an exercise in tidying up; it was a revelation. I let go of clothes I hadn't worn in years— items I had kept out of guilt or "just in case." With each piece I donated, I felt lighter, as if I were shedding layers of unnecessary weight. The space I created wasn't only physical; it was emotional. It gave me clarity, a sense of control, and the ability to focus on what truly mattered. The same happened when I organized my phone, removing apps that served no purpose and curating my digital space to reflect what was truly important to me.

Minimalism, at its heart, is valuing what you have and keeping life simple and intentional. It's a mindset that prioritizes quality over quantity, mindfulness over impulse, and clarity over chaos. When you simplify your life, you make room for what truly matters—your passions, your relationships, and your peace of mind.

As you embrace these steps, you'll find that less truly is more. The space you create—physically, mentally, and emotionally—becomes a foundation for happiness. By clearing the unnecessary, you open yourself to the things that bring lasting joy.

When you embrace the mentality of minimalism, you transform not only your surroundings but your entire perspective on happiness.

Happiness Through Less

Minimalism clears distractions, helping you focus on the people, experiences, and goals that truly matter. Clutter—whether in your physical spaces or your mind—drains your energy and clouds your focus. It's the endless pile of tasks you feel you'll never finish or the mental weight of worrying about things that barely serve you. Simplicity, on the other hand, creates room for clarity, peace, and genuine happiness.

Minimalism doesn't mean stripping your life bare. It's about valuing what serves you, letting go of what doesn't, and making thoughtful choices. When you free yourself from excess, you create space and energy for what fulfills you. It's not about restriction; it's about intentionality.

Have you ever walked into a cluttered room and felt a sense of unease you couldn't quite place? Or looked at your schedule and wondered how you'd find a moment to breathe? These moments show how clutter—physical or mental—creates tension. Simplifying eases this weight, giving you room to think, act, and live with purpose.

Start small. Choose one corner of your home or one part of your routine to simplify. Maybe it's your desk, crowded with papers you no longer need, or your wardrobe, filled with clothes you haven't worn in years. Ask yourself: does this serve a purpose? Does it align with the life I want to create? Each item or task you let go of creates space—physically and mentally—for what truly matters.

The same principle applies to how you spend your time. Are there commitments or activities that drain your energy without adding meaning to your life? By learning to say no to what doesn't align with your values, you create room for the things that do. Simplifying your schedule can be just as transformative as decluttering your home.

Minimalism naturally leads to mindfulness. When you stop chasing distractions, you're left with what's real. Imagine a quiet morning with no unnecessary errands, where you can focus on savoring a cup of tea, reflecting on your goals, or enjoying the presence of loved ones. These moments, though small, make life richer and more fulfilling.

This perspective isn't new.

Older generations often lived with less yet found immense happiness in their daily lives. They focused on relationships, meaningful work, and the joy of simple pleasures. Their stories remind us that fulfillment doesn't come from owning more but from appreciating what you already have. These lessons are worth revisiting, especially in today's fast-paced world. Imagine sitting with your family, hearing stories from grandparents about how they were happy with fewer things but deeper connections. These conversations can shift priorities, showing us the value of simplicity.

Minimalism isn't deprivation; it's abundance—not in things, but in purpose, clarity, and peace. It's recognizing what truly adds to your life, whether that's fewer possessions, a more focused schedule, or an intentional way of living. Each step toward simplicity creates space for the things that nurture you and bring joy.

This clarity paves the way for something even more meaningful: understanding yourself. With fewer distractions and a quieter mind, you can reflect on your values, your purpose, and the life you want to create.

True happiness begins where simplicity meets self-awareness.

Chapter 5

ENJOY YOUR CUP OF TEA

"Knowing others is intelligence; knowing yourself is true wisdom." – Lao Tzu

The tea was piping hot, the steam curling in delicate spirals, carrying the earthy aroma of cardamom and ginger. I sat by the window, the world outside humming with life—a distant honk, the rustle of leaves, the faint chatter of neighbors. Yet, as I held the warm cup in my hands, it felt as though the world had paused. This wasn't just tea; it was a moment of stillness, a chance to reflect.

It's surprising how rare such moments are in our busy lives. We move from one task to the next, ticking off checkboxes, answering calls, scrolling through endless feeds. The noise of life drowns out the quiet voice within, the one asking, "What truly matters to you?"

As I sipped, Lao Tzu's words echoed in my mind: "Knowing others is intelligence; knowing yourself is true wisdom." It struck me how little time we spend trying to know ourselves. We pride ourselves on understanding others—their motivations, their stories, their preferences—but how often do we pause to understand our own?

The challenge, I realized, lies in the wiring.

Our beliefs, habits, and behaviors are shaped from childhood, influenced by family, culture, and society. Unraveling these layers to find what genuinely resonates with us takes effort. It's like peeling an onion—sometimes it brings clarity, other times it brings tears. But the rewards are profound: clarity, peace, and a deeper connection to what brings us joy.

It's easy to mistake life's purpose as something grand and elusive, something that requires a dramatic quest or monumental achievement. But what if it's simpler than that? What if it begins with the small act of asking yourself, "What makes me happy?"

For years, I chased external validation—whether through work, social obligations, or even the curated perfection of online life. I told myself it was necessary, that success was measured by how others viewed me. But the more I tried to please others, the further I drifted from what truly mattered. It wasn't until I stumbled upon a quote by Epictetus that everything shifted: "In trying to please other people, we lose our hold on our life's purpose."

That line stayed with me, like a whisper in a crowded room, reminding me to pause and recalibrate. What if I stopped trying to meet everyone else's expectations? What if happiness wasn't something I earned through achievements or accolades but something I could cultivate by aligning my life with my own values?

This shift didn't happen overnight. It began with questions—simple yet transformative ones: What brings me joy? What impact do I want to create? How would I like to be remembered? Each answer felt like a piece of a puzzle, slowly forming a clearer picture of who I was and what I wanted my life to be.

I invite you to take a moment and ask yourself these questions. Not with the pressure of finding the perfect answer, but with the curiosity of someone rediscovering a forgotten treasure. What if your purpose wasn't something to chase but something already within you, waiting to be uncovered?

As we explore this journey of self-awareness, we'll see how letting go of negativity and embracing intentionality can clear the path for growth. But for now, take another sip of tea and let these questions linger. Sometimes, the answers come when you least expect them.

Steering Clear of Negativity

Have you ever found yourself in a conversation, nodding along as the topic shifts to someone else's life—their choices, mistakes, or misfortunes? At first, it might feel harmless, even bonding. But if you pause for a moment and step back, you'll notice something unsettling: the more the conversation focuses on tearing others down, the heavier it starts to feel. Gossip, often cloaked as harmless chatter, has a way of quietly poisoning our minds and draining our energy.

Let's start by unpacking what gossip really is. The Oxford Dictionary defines it as "informal talk about other people and their private lives, that is often unkind or untrue." Vocabulary.com adds that it's "conversation that's light, informal, and usually about other people's business." On the surface, it may seem like an easy way to connect with others or pass time. But beneath this facade lies its toxic nature, which can erode not only relationships but also your sense of self.

Gossip creates a cycle of negativity. When we engage in it, we focus on what's wrong with others instead of nurturing empathy or understanding. It can chip away at our self-esteem, leaving us anxious or even depressed. Worse, it's a monumental waste of time—time that could have been spent on growth, connection, or simply enjoying life.

You might wonder, why do people gossip? It's easy to think it's something "they" do, but the truth is, most of us have fallen into the trap at some point. Gossip often stems from a need for social bonding or validation. For some, it's entertainment; for others, it's a way to feel included in a group. Sometimes, it's even a misguided attempt to deal with insecurity—poking into someone else's life to distract from one's own struggles. But when gossip becomes a habit, it doesn't take long for its harmful effects to spread.

Let me share two stories that highlight how gossip can spiral into something far more damaging than it first appears.

The first took place during a function back in the year 2007-08. It was a group of college going students—young but mature enough to handle responsibility, or so we thought. The trip had been planned meticulously, and everyone was excited. But on the morning of departure, one of the friends could not catch the bus due to some reason. This was back the time when people had mobile phones but not everyone atleast at the time of college so someone said, "Why don't we just go to his hostel and check on him?" But nobody stepped up, and the bus ended up leaving without him. The next day, when he asked why he hadn't been called, a gossip-lover among the group told him an entirely fabricated story. The boy believed it, and it led to months of tension and broken friendships. It wasn't until three months later, after he confronted his friends, that the truth came out. By then, the damage had already been done.

The second story is about a girl who quite literally, thrived on gossip. She loved being the center of attention, spinning stories and dissecting others' lives. But when her circumstances changed—a move to a new place with no familiar faces—she found herself isolated. The habit she had leaned on for years didn't serve her anymore. With no one to gossip with, she became withdrawn and depressed. It was only after reflecting on her behavior and breaking the habit that she began to heal.

Both stories reveal the deeper truth about gossip: it's not only harmful to the subject but also to the person engaging in it. Gossip fosters distrust, damages relationships, and perpetuates negativity. It's a habit that might start with small talk but can quickly spiral into something far more destructive.

So, how do we steer clear of this negativity? The first step is awareness. Pay attention to your conversations. Are they building people up or tearing them down? If you catch yourself slipping into gossip, pause and redirect the conversation. Instead of focusing on someone else's shortcomings, talk about solutions, share uplifting stories, or discuss your own goals and growth.

Healthy communication is the antidote to gossip.

It's about choosing kindness over judgment and connection over division. It's about leading by example - making an environment where people feel safe and valued rather than scrutinized. If you find yourself in a group conversation heading into gossip territory, be the one to shift the tone. Ask a thoughtful question or share something positive. You'll be surprised how quickly others follow your lead.

This isn't to say we should never discuss challenges or concerns. But there's a difference between seeking support and indulging in negativity. When we approach conversations with empathy and a focus on solutions, we create opportunities for growth and connection instead of perpetuating harm.

As you sip your tea and reflect, think about this: what kind of conversations do you want to cultivate? What impact do you want your words to have—on others and on yourself? By steering clear of gossip and negativity, you're not only protecting your own happiness but also creating a ripple effect of positivity in the lives of those around you.

This is where true connection begins—not in the tearing down, but in the building up.

Practicing Self-Love

The tea was gone, but its warmth lingered, much like the thoughts it had stirred. Self-awareness, I realized, is only the beginning. The real work begins when we turn that understanding inward, learning to not only know ourselves but to embrace what we find. This is the essence of self-love—a journey that starts with acceptance and grows into care and respect for who we are, just as we are.

I once met an elderly woman who ran a small mess for students, and her story has stayed with me. Her setup was modest—30 students, no more, no less. This wasn't due to a lack of ambition but a deliberate choice. "I want to maintain the quality," she said. "Cooking is my passion, and feeding students reminds me of home. It's about doing what I love with care and intention."

Her space was warm and inviting, decorated with simple touches that made it feel like a second home for those young students far from their families. She spoke with pride about how some of her former students, now with families of their own, still visited her mess to share a meal and relive their memories. "That," she said with a smile, "is my real reward."

Her story wasn't just about cooking; it was a testament to self-love in action. She had set clear boundaries, choosing to focus on quality over quantity. She found joy in the act of giving and took pride in maintaining her routine. Her self-love wasn't loud or showy—it was quiet, steady, and deeply rooted in her values.

This, I realized, is what self-love looks like. It's not about perfection or grand gestures. It's in the small things: setting boundaries that protect your peace, celebrating your growth—whether it's a small victory or a major milestone—and creating time for yourself amidst life's demands.

When was the last time you rewarded yourself for a job well done? Maybe it was something as simple as enjoying your favorite meal, taking a long walk, or buying a book you've been meaning to read. These acts of self-appreciation aren't indulgences; they're affirmations. They're ways of telling yourself, "I see you. I value you."

Self-love also means learning to say no—to people, to situations, to anything that drains your energy or pulls you away from your values. It's not always easy, especially when saying yes feels more convenient. But every time you say no to something that doesn't serve you, you're saying yes to yourself.

And then there's gratitude. When was the last time you thanked yourself? Not for something extraordinary, but for simply showing up, trying, and persevering? Gratitude isn't only for others; it's for you too. It's a way to acknowledge your efforts, honor your journey, and remind yourself of your worth.

As I walked away from that little mess, my stomach full and my heart fuller, I couldn't help but smile. Her story wasn't just inspiring; it was a reminder that self-love isn't a destination. It's a practice, a daily act of kindness directed inward. It's in the way you talk to yourself, the choices you make, and the boundaries you set. It shapes how you move through the world, making each step lighter and more purposeful.

And as you pour your next cup of tea, take a moment to ask yourself: What would self-love look like for you today? Maybe it's setting aside five minutes to breathe, reaching out to a friend who lifts your spirits, or simply saying, "I did my best, and that's enough." Whatever it is, let it be a step toward embracing the person you are and the person you're becoming.

Self-love is not a luxury; it's a necessity. It's the foundation of happiness, and it starts with one small, intentional choice at a time.

So take that step—because you deserve it.

Self-love leads naturally to mindfulness, where the focus shifts from understanding oneself to embracing each moment with intention and clarity. It's this mindful connection that creates a bridge between introspection and purposeful living, paving the way for deeper joy and lasting peace.

Mindfulness in Action

The world outside seemed to hum with its usual rhythm—cars passing, birds chirping, the occasional chatter from neighbors. But inside, everything was quiet. This was a deliberate pause, a choice to disconnect from the noise and reconnect with myself.

Mindfulness is often described as the secret medicine of happiness, and I'd come to understand why. It wasn't emptying the mind or achieving some lofty ideal; it was simply creating space—to observe, to reflect, and to act with intention.

Mindfulness, at its core, is a bridge. It connects introspection—the quiet understanding of oneself—with purposeful action. It's what transforms awareness into change, ideas into habits, and moments into meaning. It's not instantaneous, but its power lies in its consistency. Like drops of water carving a stone, mindfulness reshapes the way we see, think, and respond to the world around us.

A friend of mine taught me this lesson in a way I'll never forget. He was the kind of person who lived impulsively, charging through life without pause. His language was harsh, his habits reckless, and his relationships strained. On paper, he had everything: a well-paying job, a newly purchased home, a loving partner. But beneath the surface, he was lost. I remember the day he finally opened up to me. His voice wavered as he described feeling stuck, disconnected, and deeply unhappy.

"What do you think I should do?" he asked, almost pleading.

"Start with yourself," I told him. "You're carrying so much, but you've never stopped to ask why."

We worked out a plan—a simple, intentional routine to help him understand and untangle his thoughts. The first step was journaling. For ten days, he wrote down everything that came to mind—no filters, no judgments. Each evening, he'd go back through his entries, identifying patterns and sorting out which thoughts lifted him up and which ones dragged him down.

The next phase was about asking the right questions. For ten days, he focused on prompts like: "What brings me real joy?" "What are my core values?" "Where do I want to go from here?" "What am I most passionate about?" These questions weren't about finding immediate answers; they were about sparking curiosity and clarity.

By the third phase, he was ready to start letting go. He began addressing the negative habits that had been holding him back, replacing them with healthier routines. He committed to a 30-minute daily meditation practice, which, at first, felt like a monumental task. But with time, he found solace in the stillness. He began observing his thoughts without judgment, letting the noise settle so he could focus on what truly mattered.

Three months later, the transformation was undeniable. He was calmer, more organized, and genuinely happier. His girlfriend even thanked me, sharing how his newfound mindfulness had strengthened their relationship. "He's not impulsive anymore," she said. "It's like he finally sees what's important."

This is the power of mindfulness. It doesn't demand perfection. It doesn't expect you to erase every flaw or quiet every doubt. Instead, it invites you to show up—for yourself, for your thoughts, and for your life. It's a practice, not a destination, and each step forward brings its own rewards.

How can you bring mindfulness into your life?

Start with time and space. Choose a moment in your day—perhaps first thing in the morning or just before bed—to sit quietly and reflect. Journal your thoughts - without censoring them. Write down what made you smile, what challenged you, and what you wish to improve. Over time, these reflections become a map to your inner self.

Ask yourself questions that matter. Not the "what-ifs" that lead to worry, but the "what's next" that lead to growth. What excites you? What holds you back? What are you ready to let go of? These questions are keys, unlocking doors to parts of yourself you might not have explored.

Meditation is another powerful tool. Contrary to popular belief, it's not about emptying your mind; it's about focusing it. Sit comfortably, close your eyes, and take deep breaths. As thoughts arise—and they will—acknowledge them without clinging to them. Let them pass, like clouds drifting across the sky. With practice, you'll find a sense of clarity and calm that extends beyond those moments of stillness.

Mindfulness is a journey, one that requires patience and commitment. But the changes it brings are profound. It helps you respond thoughtfully rather than react impulsively. It creates space for gratitude, for self-love, and for purpose. And most importantly, it reminds you that happiness isn't something to chase; it's something to cultivate, one mindful moment at a time.

This practice embodies the true meaning of enjoying your cup of tea. It's an invitation to slow down, connect with yourself, and find depth in the small, intentional acts that make up life. It's not defined by grand gestures or unattainable ideals but by being present in every moment—one sip, one thought, and one breath at a time. As you hold your cup and feel its warmth, let it serve as a gentle reminder to embrace life's simplicity, savor its richness, and uncover happiness in its quiet beauty.

Mindfulness challenges us to live each day with intention—to engage with our thoughts, actions, and connections with a sense of clarity and purpose.

The answers to how you can live this way already lie within you, waiting to be discovered.

All you need to do is pause, reflect, and begin.

Chapter 6

REACT OR RESPOND?

"Between stimulus and response there is a space. In that space is our power to choose our response. In our response lies our growth and our freedom."
– Viktor E. Frankl

This quote captures a truth so simple yet profound—it's in the small spaces of our daily lives where the biggest transformations occur. But what does that space look like in practice? Sometimes, it appears in the split-second decisions we face, like during an ordinary drive on a Tuesday afternoon.

The car in front came to an abrupt halt, forcing me to slam on the brakes. My heart raced as the tires screeched, narrowly avoiding a collision. My instinct was to honk, roll down the window, and let my frustration spill out in a few choice words. But just as I reached for the horn, something held me back. In the silence of that brief moment, I felt a small but powerful space open up.

What would reacting accomplish? Would it ease the tension in my chest or fix the situation? Or would it escalate things, turning a fleeting inconvenience into a memory I'd later regret? Instead of reacting, I took a deep breath, exhaled slowly, and let it go. The car moved forward, and so did I—literally and emotionally.

That space between stimulus and response, as Viktor Frankl so beautifully described, is where our power lies. In those moments, we decide who we are and how we show up. Will we let circumstances dictate our behavior, or will we take a beat to think, reflect, and respond intentionally?

Psychology tells us that reactions are instinctive. They're fast, automatic, and often driven by past experiences or raw emotions. Responses, on the other hand, require thought. They're deliberate, considerate, and shaped by awareness of the bigger picture. The difference between the two can feel subtle in the moment, but its impact on our happiness and relationships is profound.

Think about the last time you reacted impulsively—a heated argument, a rushed decision, or even a careless remark. Did it make the situation better, or did it leave you wishing you'd paused? Now consider a time when you took a moment to breathe, to think, to choose your words or actions carefully. How did that change the outcome? How did it feel afterward?

This chapter is about exploring that space and learning to expand it. It's about understanding the power we hold in every situation, no matter how small or significant. Through thoughtful responses, we not only shape our immediate environment but also cultivate long-term peace and happiness.

So what does it mean to respond, instead of react, and how can focusing on response transform the way we experience the world?

Reactions vs. Responses

Reactions are fast, automatic, and instinctive.

They arise almost immediately, fueled by emotions like anger, fear, or frustration. Often, they are rooted in past experiences or deep-seated fears. Imagine someone saying something unkind about you, and you snap back with equal anger and harsh words. In that moment, your reaction feels justified—even necessary—but does it truly serve you? Reactions are driven by the heat of the moment and rarely consider the long-term effects or consequences.

Take, for example, Newton's law: every action has an equal and opposite reaction. While it's a principle that governs physics, many of us unknowingly apply it to emotional situations. Someone cuts you off in traffic, and your immediate response is frustration, perhaps even anger. You honk, shout, or glare. Does it fix the situation, or does it leave you more agitated? Reactions often escalate conflicts instead of resolving them, leaving a trail of stress and regret.

In contrast, responses are intentional and thoughtful.

They require a pause—a deliberate moment to assess the situation and decide how to proceed. Responses take into account not just the immediate circumstances but also the bigger picture. They are rooted in logic, empathy, and a desire for resolution rather than escalation.

Here's another way to think about it:

- **Reaction**: "Re" + "Act" – repeated, instinctive actions based on emotional triggers.
- **Response**: "Re" + "Sponse" – an act sponsored by thought and intention.

Let's revisit the earlier example of being cut off in traffic. Instead of immediately reacting with anger, consider taking a deep breath. Perhaps the other driver didn't see you or was in a genuine hurry. By choosing to respond thoughtfully—perhaps letting it go or safely adjusting your speed—you protect your peace of mind and avoid unnecessary stress. This small shift transforms the situation from one of frustration to one of control.

Reactions are often regretted, while responses leave room for growth, understanding, and better outcomes. They represent two entirely different approaches to life: one reactive and driven by the moment, the other proactive and guided by intentionality.

This distinction isn't limited to traffic scenarios. Think of the last time a colleague gave you feedback at work. Was your initial instinct defensive? Did you feel the urge to justify or explain yourself immediately? That's a reaction. A response, on the other hand, might involve listening, reflecting, and saying, "Thank you for the feedback. Let me think about this and get back to you." Which approach fosters better relationships and personal growth?

Becoming a responsive person takes time and practice. It starts with recognizing your triggers. What situations or comments tend to provoke immediate, unfiltered reactions? Awareness is the first step to change.

Reactions are often a result of deeply ingrained habits, but as you've probably learnt by now, habits can be reformed. Responses require a conscious effort—a choice to pause, reflect, and act with intention. Over time, this practice reshapes how we interact with the world and ourselves.

Breaking reaction habits requires deliberate effort and patience.

Expanding that space between stimulus and response opens doors to clarity, connection, and enduring peace. While the transformation isn't immediate, each thoughtful choice to respond rather than react builds resilience, balance, and a deeper sense of happiness.

Breaking Reaction Habits

"As long as you think someone or something else is responsible for the way that you are, you cannot become the way you want to be."
– Sadhguru

This idea is powerful because it shifts the responsibility squarely onto us. It's not easy to admit, but how we react isn't anyone else's doing. Blaming others or external circumstances might feel natural in the moment, but it also keeps us stuck. The first step to breaking reaction habits is acknowledging this truth: we have a choice. And that choice begins with awareness.

Reflect on a moment when frustration got the better of you—maybe during a disagreement with a colleague or a tense exchange at home. Could the outcome have been different if handled with a pause and perspective? Reactions like these often stem from unresolved triggers—past experiences, fears, or assumptions—and they pile on stress unnecessarily. Stress then becomes the fuel for more reactions, creating a cycle that feels impossible to escape.

But here's the good news: the cycle can be broken. Let me share a story.

A friend of mine, someone who'd always been described as quick-tempered, found herself constantly drained. Her stress wasn't from external situations, but from how she handled them. One day, after a heated argument over something trivial, she decided enough was enough. She began journaling her triggers. "Was it their tone? Did I feel dismissed?" These questions became her starting point. By recognizing her patterns, she started pausing before reacting. Over time, she transformed, becoming more measured and calm—not overnight, but step by step.

Breaking reaction habits isn't focused on perfection; it's focused on progress. Here are some practical steps to help you begin:

Identify Triggers

Start by noticing what sets you off. Keep a small journal or use your phone to jot down situations where you felt reactive. Was it someone cutting you off in traffic? A sharp comment from a coworker? A missed deadline? Identifying these moments is like holding a mirror to your habits—it's the first step in understanding where your energy is going.

Ask yourself:

- Was my reaction necessary?
- What emotions surfaced in that moment?
- What's the real root of my response?

Pause and Breathe

When you feel the tension rising, pause. Take a deep breath—in through your nose for four seconds, hold for four, and exhale slowly for six. This simple act calms your nervous system and gives your mind a chance to catch up with your emotions. In that pause, ask yourself: "Is this worth my energy? What outcome do I want?"

Research shows that deep breathing activates the parasympathetic nervous system, reducing stress hormones like cortisol. It's not just a quick fix; it's a powerful tool to reset your response in the heat of the moment.

Mindful Self-Talk

Your inner dialogue matters. Instead of spiraling into negative thoughts, guide yourself with questions:

- "What am I trying to achieve here?"
- "Is this the best way to handle the situation?"

Positive affirmations can also help: "I have the power to choose my response. My peace is more important than winning this argument."

Seek Feedback

Sometimes, we're too close to our habits to see them clearly. Talk to someone you trust—a family member, a friend, or a mentor. Ask for honest feedback about how you handle stress or conflict. Their perspective can be eye-opening. Remember, this isn't about judgment; it's about growth.

Celebrate Progress

Changing habits takes time, and small victories deserve recognition. The next time you pause instead of snapping, or choose silence over a heated comeback, celebrate it. Progress, however small, is still progress. Write it down, smile, and acknowledge the effort you're putting in. Each win reinforces the habit of responding thoughtfully.

These steps might feel unfamiliar at first, but with consistent practice, they become second nature. The more you choose to respond instead of react, the easier it gets. And the benefits extend far beyond individual moments—they ripple into your relationships, your peace of mind, and your overall well-being.

Think about how these principles come to life in everyday situations—whether it's managing workplace tensions or dealing with conflicts on the road. Practicing calm responses can transform even the most challenging moments into opportunities for growth and understanding.

Everyday Scenarios

Life is full of moments that test your patience.

Whether it's a chaotic morning commute, a tense workplace meeting, or a frustrating exchange with customer service, the opportunities to react impulsively are endless. But here's the good news: each of these moments is also a chance to practice responding thoughtfully and constructively.

I'll give you an example: a situation we all encounter - traffic.

Picture this: It's the end of a long day, and you're driving home, eager to unwind. The roads are congested, with cars crawling bumper-to-bumper. Suddenly, a vehicle swerves into your lane, forcing you to slam the brakes. Your heart races, and frustration bubbles to the surface.

What would you do?

There are two possible ways you could go about this: "Re-act" and "Re-spond."

Re-act: The car cuts you off, and your anger surges. Your horn blares, and you shout words the driver can't hear. As the irritation lingers, you replay the incident in your head. By the time you arrive home, the tension hasn't dissipated. Instead of enjoying your evening, you feel on edge, letting a single moment overshadow your peace.

Re-spond: The same car cuts you off, but this time, you pause. You grip the wheel tightly for a moment, then take a deep breath. You remind yourself, "What will honking achieve? Is it worth carrying this anger home?" As you exhale, you turn your attention back to the song playing on the radio. By the time you pull into your driveway, the incident is a distant memory, and your mood remains intact.

This contrast isn't theoretical—it's something most of us experience regularly. Traffic challenges us to manage our emotions, but it also offers opportunities to practice intentional responses. As discussed earlier, "Re-act" stems from impulse and emotion, while "Re-spond" carries the sponsorship of thought.

Choosing to respond shifts not only the moment but sets a positive tone for the entire trajectory of your day.

It's these small, mindful choices that shape a more fulfilling life, and the overall quality of it.

Let's consider another everyday scenario: workplace feedback.

Feedback—whether it's constructive or critical—is a common trigger for reactions. A colleague points out an error in your work during a meeting. Do you bristle defensively, jumping to justify yourself, or do you take a moment to absorb their words before responding?

I once worked with someone who struggled deeply with criticism. Every piece of feedback felt like a personal attack, and their immediate reactions—sharp retorts, visible frustration—only created tension in the office.

Over time, they realized this pattern was isolating them from colleagues and increasing their stress. By focusing on responding instead of reacting, they transformed their relationships at work. Instead of snapping back, they began saying, "Thank you for pointing that out. Let me think it over and get back to you." This shift not only improved their professional interactions but also their confidence and peace of mind.

Each moment where tension could arise became an opportunity to practice calm responses.

Let's shift focus to another scenario that's all too familiar: customer service.

Imagine this: a delayed order, an overcharged bill, or an unhelpful customer service representative. These situations test our patience, and frustration might feel like the easiest reaction. But what happens if you pause instead and approach with patience and empathy?

I recall an incident at a store where a billing mistake led to a heated exchange. The customer ahead of me was raising their voice, and the cashier looked visibly stressed. When it was my turn, I noticed the tension in the air. Instead of reacting to the long wait or potential errors, I began by saying, "It's been a busy day for you, hasn't it?"

That simple acknowledgment shifted the tone entirely. The cashier smiled, and we resolved the issue quickly and calmly. Responding with kindness doesn't just ease your stress—it can transform someone else's day as well. Empathy is the bridge that connects understanding to action. It allows us to see beyond the immediate conflict and into the human side of every interaction.

Practicing empathy doesn't mean suppressing your emotions or avoiding conflict altogether.

Instead, it's about redirecting your feelings in a way that fosters connection and understanding. Take the example of a traffic jam—when irritation mounts, stopping to recognize that everyone else on the road might be experiencing their own frustrations can shift your outlook. In a workplace setting, feedback that feels critical might come from a place of genuine concern or collaboration. Empathy enables you to look past the tone and see the intent. Similarly, in a customer service issue, taking a moment to acknowledge the challenges faced by the person assisting you can turn an otherwise tense interaction into a shared effort to resolve the problem constructively. Empathy transforms these everyday moments from sources of friction into opportunities for meaningful connection and mutual respect.

Ask yourself: "What's the bigger picture here? What's the best outcome for everyone involved?" These questions help ground you, shifting your focus from immediate frustration to meaningful resolution. By practicing empathy, you not only diffuse tension but also strengthen your ability to connect, adapt, and grow.

When you approach situations with a calm mind and an open heart, you're not just managing the moment—you're building emotional intelligence and resilience. Each thoughtful response reinforces habits that lead to long-term happiness and healthier relationships.

Take these lessons with you as you face the everyday challenges of life. The next time you're in a stressful situation, pause and think about whether you want to RE-act or RE-spond.

Remember, your response has the power to change the outcome—not just for that moment, but for the person you're becoming.

When you pause to consider your next move, you're not just avoiding a hasty reaction—you're creating space for growth, for understanding, and for change. This intentional choice opens doors to a more thoughtful and connected life.

But how do we take this practice deeper and foster a mindset that supports calm responses in every aspect of life? That's where self-awareness and intentional techniques come in—shaping not just how we respond, but who we become in the process.

Fostering Calm Responses

"Being ignored is a great privilege. That is how I think I learned to see what others do not see and to react to situations differently." — Saul Leiter

There's something disarming about feeling overlooked, isn't there?

In the moment, it might sting—the absence of acknowledgment, the sense of being invisible. But what if that silence holds an unexpected gift? What if it's an invitation to step back, reflect, and grow?

I remember a time when I felt adrift in a group setting. Surrounded by conversations and laughter, I felt disconnected. My initial instinct was resentment—to withdraw emotionally or lash out with frustration. But then, a thought struck me: What if this wasn't rejection but an opportunity? Instead of reacting, I used that time to focus inward. I asked myself questions I'd never taken the time to consider. Why did I feel this way? Was the group's validation what I truly sought, or was this a chance to understand myself better?

That moment sparked a practice that changed my perspective. I began seeing solitude—even unchosen solitude—as a space for growth. The more I leaned into self-awareness, the more I understood how much of my emotional turmoil came from reacting impulsively to situations. With time, I learned that being ignored wasn't rejection; it was an opportunity to connect with myself.

Techniques for Fostering Calm Responses

Calm responses aren't about bottling up emotions or pretending everything is fine. They're about approaching situations with clarity and intention. Here are some techniques that can help:

1. Journaling with Clarity

What does it mean to foster calm responses? It starts with understanding your patterns. One of the most transformative tools I discovered was journalizing—a combination of journaling and analyzing. Alongside my daily reflections, I created two columns: "I Reacted" and "I Responded." Each night, I would revisit the day's events and jot down moments where I acted impulsively versus thoughtfully. Over time, patterns emerged. I began to see what triggered my reactions and what allowed me to respond thoughtfully.

This practice isn't about self-criticism. It's about awareness. By shining a light on our tendencies, we gain the power to change them. And when you track your progress, even small victories—like pausing before responding to a sharp comment—feel monumental.

Think of this as a guidebook to your emotions, helping you navigate challenging moments with intention.

2. Know Yourself

Self-awareness is the foundation of calm responses. Start by identifying your emotional triggers. Is it criticism? Feeling unheard? A sense of injustice? Understanding what sets you off gives you a head start in managing those moments. Pair this with recognizing your strengths. Knowing what keeps you grounded—whether it's humor, patience, or empathy—can help you lean into those qualities when challenges arise.

For example, if you know that feeling dismissed makes you reactive, you can prepare yourself to approach those situations differently. Self-awareness transforms potential triggers into opportunities for growth.

3. Practice Observation

Before reacting, take a step back and observe.

What's really happening? Is the other person angry, stressed, or simply distracted? Observation creates a buffer, allowing you to understand the situation fully before acting. It's a small pause, but it holds immense power.

Imagine watching a scene from the outside—detached and objective. This distance can reveal nuances you might miss in the heat of the moment. Observation isn't just about the other person; it's also about checking in with yourself. Are you tired, overwhelmed, or holding onto unrelated frustration? Recognizing this can shift how you choose to respond.

4. Empathy as a Tool

Empathy transforms interactions.

When someone lashes out, it's often a reflection of their own struggles. Pausing to consider their perspective doesn't excuse their behavior but helps you respond with understanding instead of escalation. Imagine being in their shoes—what might they be feeling? What would you hope for in their place?

Empathy doesn't mean agreeing with someone or letting go of your boundaries. It means responding in a way that prioritizes connection over conflict. A kind word or a calm tone can shift the entire dynamic of a conversation. Think of empathy as a bridge—it doesn't erase differences, but it connects you to a place of mutual understanding.

For instance, a colleague's harsh tone might stem from stress at home rather than frustration with you.

Recognizing this can soften your response and transform the interaction.

5. Learn from Every Experience

Every situation—good or bad—has something to teach us.

Reflect on moments where you reacted impulsively. What could have been done differently? Celebrate the times you responded thoughtfully. Each experience adds to your understanding and builds the foundation for better interactions in the future.

Mistakes aren't failures; they're lessons. By approaching them with curiosity rather than judgment, you create space to grow. Ask yourself: "What did I learn here?" and "How can I apply this next time?"

This mindset turns setbacks into stepping stones.

Fostering calm responses isn't about perfection. It's about progress. Each time you choose to respond instead of react, you're strengthening the muscle of emotional resilience. This effort compounds over time, creating a version of yourself that's more grounded, more empathetic, and more in control.

Calm responses build emotional resilience not just in the moment but over time. When you approach challenges with patience and understanding, you strengthen the foundation of your inner peace. This resilience becomes the bedrock of healthier relationships, improved well-being, and a stronger connection with yourself.

Think about it: When you respond calmly, you're not just managing the immediate situation—you're shaping your long-term well-being. The ripple effects touch every area of your life, from your relationships to your personal sense of peace. Choosing calm isn't always easy, but it's always worth it.

So the next time you feel that surge of frustration or impatience, pause. Take a breath. Ask yourself: What outcome do I want here? And what choice will align with the person I want to be?

Responding thoughtfully transforms not only the moment but also your journey.

It builds connections, cultivates peace, and strengthens your relationship with yourself. It's a practice worth embracing—one moment, one response at a time.

Chapter 7

IT'S OKAY TO BE AVERAGE

"Average."

What does this word bring to mind?

If you find yourself thinking back to your school days, you are not alone.

Remember the day report cards were handed out? Parents whispering to each other, comparing grades. Or family gatherings where conversations veered toward a cousin's gold medal, a neighbor's perfect score, or the relentless question, "What rank did you get?" How often did you hear, "Don't settle for being average"? These words, often said with good intentions, carried an undertone of disappointment, an expectation to stand out, to shine.

But what does it truly mean to be "average"? And why does it feel so heavy? In many Indian homes, "average" becomes a shorthand for not measuring up, for blending into the background.

Yet, what if we saw it differently?

What if average wasn't a label of failure but a position of possibility?

Average is not a final verdict; it's a midpoint, a space filled with potential. It's the balance between where you've been and where you're going.

John Wooden once said, "Being average means you are as close to the bottom as you are to the top." It's a powerful reminder that being average isn't the end of the story—it's the point where the next chapter begins. It's a place where you can pause, recalibrate, and decide your next move—whether it's striving for progress, finding contentment, or a mix of both.

Think of a sportsperson—someone who reaches the peak of their game but then faces a slump in form. In that moment, they're called "average." But does that define them? Hardly. It's in those times that they return to the basics, rediscover their strengths, and push forward. Average, in this sense, isn't a failure; it's a reset.

It's where resilience begins.

In our quest for perfection—whether in academics, careers, or relationships—we often overlook the beauty of the journey. The pressure to excel can rob us of the joy found in small wins and steady progress. Being "average" doesn't mean giving up; it means recognizing where you are and valuing the journey as much as the destination. It's finding joy in the process while staying focused on where you want to go.

So, what if you could shift your perspective on "average"? What if it wasn't something to avoid but a mindset to embrace—a space for growth, balance, and renewed purpose? Let's see how redefining "average" can transform not only your outlook but your entire approach to life.

The Joy of Modest Goals

In a world that glorifies constant achievement and relentless ambition, the idea of setting modest goals might seem underwhelming. But there's a quiet power in starting small, in defining targets that are both realistic and achievable.

Think back to any time you felt overwhelmed by a daunting task—whether it was a complex project at work, preparing for an important exam, or even something as personal as getting back into shape after years of neglect. The enormity of the end goal often creates paralysis, leaving us stuck and discouraged.

But what if, instead, you broke those intimidating objectives into smaller, manageable steps?

Take, for example, a friend of mine who once aspired to run a marathon. For months, she would buy running gear, research training schedules, and visualize crossing the finish line, but she never took the first step—literally.

The marathon seemed too far, too overwhelming. Then, one day, she shifted her approach. Instead of focusing on the marathon, she set a simpler goal: running for five minutes a day. That was it. Five minutes. She built from there—ten minutes the following week, then fifteen. Within six months, she wasn't just running; she was thriving. Small, consistent efforts led her to the very achievement that once felt unattainable.

Setting modest goals doesn't mean lowering your aspirations. It means creating a plan that's realistic and sustainable.

When you start small, you create opportunities for early wins—those moments of achievement that build confidence and momentum. Each success, however small, reminds you that progress is possible and keeps you motivated to continue. These milestones don't just bring joy; they transform the journey itself into something fulfilling.

If you're wondering how to set modest goals for yourself, start with where you are right now.

Consider your daily routines, your strengths, and the areas you'd like to grow in. For instance, if your long-term goal is to master a new language, don't begin by committing to two-hour study sessions every day. Start with a simple, actionable plan: ten minutes of vocabulary practice or listening to a podcast in that language during your commute. These manageable steps create a foundation for consistency, which is far more powerful than bursts of unsustainable effort.

This approach also encourages better time management. By focusing on smaller goals, you can integrate them seamlessly into your daily life without feeling overwhelmed. A modest goal doesn't demand perfection; it invites you to show up as you are and make progress in meaningful increments. It's this focus that leads to consistent growth and improvement.

Think of the Bruce Lee quote: "A successful warrior is an average man, with a laser-like focus." Success doesn't come from monumental leaps; it comes from small, deliberate steps taken with unwavering focus. Modest goals sharpen your ability to concentrate on what truly matters while eliminating the distractions that often accompany overly ambitious targets.

When you start to achieve these smaller milestones, something magical happens: you begin to enjoy the process. Achievements are no longer distant peaks to be scaled but moments of joy that punctuate your everyday life. You find yourself celebrating progress, no matter how incremental, and that celebration fuels further growth. This shift in perspective allows you to focus not only on where you're going but also on how far you've come.

This joy of modest goals ties seamlessly into the broader exploration of finding happiness in diverse interests and personal growth. As we'll see next, these smaller targets aren't confined to professional ambitions or long-term plans. They extend into every facet of life, including the hobbies and passions that bring daily joy and fulfillment.

Exploring Diverse Hobbies

Have you ever watched someone light up when they talk about their hobbies? It could be a neighbor who tends to their garden with unwavering dedication or a colleague who spends weekends strumming a guitar. These moments remind us that life's richness often lies not in grand achievements but in the smaller joys we create for ourselves.

A friend of mine embodies this beautifully. His day job is demanding, but his evenings and weekends are a patchwork of diverse pursuits. He's no master of any single craft, but he's dabbled in many—playing the keyboard, fixing gadgets, reading novels, and even trying his hand at badminton. Each activity offers something different: a mental challenge, a physical outlet, or a simple moment of peace.

One evening, after sharing his latest gadget repair success, he told me, "I don't do these things to be perfect. I do them because they make me happy. Whether it's learning a new tune or fixing a loose wire, it's satisfying to know I've done something on my own." His words stayed with me. They were a reminder that hobbies aren't about mastery but fulfillment. They're about exploring new territories, building confidence, and finding pockets of joy in our everyday lives.

Variety enriches our perspective. When you try your hand at something new—be it crafting, baking, or gardening—you open yourself to fresh experiences and knowledge. Each hobby brings with it a unique lens through which to view the world. For instance, learning to play an instrument not only develops a skill but also deepens your appreciation for music. Similarly, engaging in outdoor activities like hiking or cycling helps you reconnect with nature and build physical stamina.

Hobbies also serve as a powerful tool for stress relief. Life's demands can leave us feeling overwhelmed, but immersing yourself in a beloved activity can be like hitting the reset button. Whether it's the meditative rhythm of knitting, the adrenaline rush of a sport, or the quiet focus of sketching, hobbies offer an emotional outlet and a mental refresh.

Take the example of my friend again. On days when work feels particularly draining, he turns to music or books. "When I'm low, I play a few tunes on my keyboard," he said. "If I need physical activity, I grab my cricket bat and head to the park. These little escapes keep me grounded." His approach is a testament to how hobbies can bring balance and joy to our lives, even amidst chaos.

So, how do you begin exploring diverse hobbies? Start by asking yourself a simple question: What have you always wanted to try? Perhaps it's learning to bake, picking up a paintbrush, or joining a local sports club. The key is to approach it without the pressure of perfection. Your goal isn't to become a master but to enjoy the process of learning and growing.

Hobbies can also evolve over time.

You might start with something simple, like photography on your phone, and later find yourself experimenting with advanced techniques. Or you could begin with an interest in cooking and gradually develop a flair for creating fusion dishes. The beauty of hobbies lies in their flexibility—they grow with you, adapting to your interests and needs.

When you engage in hobbies, you're not only nurturing your personal growth but also creating a toolkit for unwinding. These activities become anchors, grounding you during stressful times and reminding you of the simple joys that life has to offer. They're a way to celebrate yourself—your curiosity, your creativity, and your resilience.

As you explore these hobbies, you'll notice something else: they often lead to unexpected connections. Joining a book club might introduce you to people with similar interests. Trying out a team sport could foster camaraderie and teamwork. Even solitary hobbies, like painting or writing, can open doors to online communities where people share tips, stories, and encouragement.

The joy of diverse hobbies is in their ability to enrich every aspect of your life. They're not distractions from your goals but companions to your journey, adding depth, perspective, and a sense of accomplishment to your days.

They remind you that growth isn't always reaching the top— sometimes, it's savoring the climb.

Recognizing this helps us shift our focus from chasing the extraordinary to appreciating the steady rhythm of progress.

Balance Through Realism

Ambition is often celebrated as the hallmark of success. We're told to dream big, aim higher, and settle for nothing less than perfection. But in this relentless chase, many of us lose sight of what really matters: balance. True growth comes not from pushing ourselves to the brink but from embracing who we are today while striving for progress tomorrow.

I once knew a colleague who was the epitome of ambition. Every goal was bigger than the last, every success a stepping stone to something grander. Yet, instead of happiness, he often seemed stressed and unfulfilled. One day, after missing an important family gathering because he was preparing for a high-stakes project, he confided in me: "I feel like I'm always running, but I don't know where I'm going." That was his turning point. He began setting more realistic goals, celebrating small victories, and rediscovering the joy in his daily life. Slowly but surely, he found a rhythm that worked for him—one rooted in balance and contentment.

Realism doesn't mean settling for mediocrity. It's about recognizing that you're a work in progress and that progress is more meaningful than perfection. Average doesn't imply a lack of ambition or drive. It means grounding your aspirations in reality and recognizing the importance of steady, sustainable growth as part of a fulfilling life.

The foundation of balance is self-awareness and acceptance. Acknowledge where you are today without judgment. This doesn't mean giving up on your goals; it means approaching them with kindness toward yourself. Imagine a plant—you don't expect it to bloom overnight. You water it, provide sunlight, and patiently nurture it. Why should your personal growth be any different?

Take a moment to assess your priorities. What truly matters to you? Write them down, separating them into personal and professional aspects. If you've made even the smallest progress toward these priorities, celebrate it. Maybe you managed to finish a report ahead of schedule, or you carved out time for a walk with family. These moments are worth acknowledging because they're stepping stones to something greater.

And when setbacks happen—as they inevitably will—be kind to yourself. Failure isn't the opposite of success; it's part of the journey. What defines you is how you respond. With flexibility and resilience, you can bounce back quickly, often stronger than before. As I said, being "average" means you're adaptable and agile, ready to tackle whatever comes your way.

Have you ever noticed how children approach failure? They fall, cry for a moment, and then get back up as if nothing happened. That's the beauty of resilience. When you're not fixated on being perfect, you allow yourself the freedom to fail and learn. This flexibility makes it easier to adapt to challenges and move forward.

Think of a time when you faced a setback. Maybe you missed a deadline, made a mistake at work, or experienced personal disappointment. How did you handle it? Did you dwell on the failure, or did you see it as an opportunity to grow? Resilience isn't about ignoring your emotions; it's about processing them, learning from the experience, and trying again.

Perfectionism often blinds us to the progress we're making. We're so focused on the end goal that we forget to enjoy the journey. But when you shift your perspective to celebrate small wins, every step forward becomes a source of joy.

Let's say you've been working toward a healthier lifestyle. Instead of fixating on losing a specific number of pounds, celebrate the fact that you went for a walk today or chose a nutritious meal. These small achievements build momentum, boosting your confidence and motivation. Over time, they lead to significant, sustainable change.

Progress isn't linear, and it's rarely perfect. Embrace the detours and delays as part of the process. These moments of resilience and self-kindness remind us that life is less about perfection and more about learning to adapt and thrive through each experience. By focusing on what you've accomplished rather than what's left to do, you cultivate a mindset of gratitude and positivity.

Balance through realism isn't a one-time achievement; it's an ongoing practice. It's the art of striving without stressing, progressing without pressuring, and succeeding without sacrificing your well-being. When you embrace this approach, you'll find that happiness isn't something to chase—it's something you create, one step at a time.

This journey of balance and self-awareness is not one we take alone. Often, the most valuable lessons come from observing those around us—everyday individuals who demonstrate the beauty of steady growth and meaningful impact.

Inspiration doesn't always come from those who achieve the extraordinary.

Often, it's the everyday individuals—those who balance their aspirations with contentment—who teach us the most about living a fulfilling life.

Inspiration from Everyday Individuals

The world often celebrates those who achieve extraordinary feats—athletes breaking records, innovators disrupting industries, or artists creating timeless masterpieces. Yet, the people who leave a lasting impression on our lives are often the ones who live quietly, focused on their passions and priorities, unburdened by the need to chase perfection.

One such individual who comes to mind is the tea vendor we met earlier. If you recall, his life—by many societal standards—might be considered "average." He wasn't leading a multi-crore business or making headlines, yet his presence radiated contentment. Each day, he poured his heart into brewing tea, perfecting a craft that brought warmth to countless customers. For him, happiness wasn't about achieving grand milestones; it was about finding purpose in the routine and joy in serving others.

When I asked him about his life, his response was simple: "I'm happy. My work keeps me connected to people, and I sleep peacefully at night knowing I've done my best." Was his life "average" by society's standards? Perhaps. But was it fulfilling? Absolutely. His story challenges the notion that happiness is tied to external achievements. It's a reminder that true success lies in alignment with your values and passions.

Then there was a friend of mine, a highly skilled engineer who achieved significant milestones in his career. Despite his accomplishments, he often referred to himself as "average." One day, I asked him why he chose this word, despite his evident expertise and success. "Because," he explained, "if I ever think I'm perfect, I'll stop learning. Being 'average' keeps me curious. It reminds me that there's always room to grow."

His humility was striking, but what stood out even more was his approach to growth. He celebrated small improvements, whether mastering a new software tool or mentoring a junior colleague. For him, "average" wasn't a limitation; it was a mindset that fostered curiosity and resilience. And that's a lesson worth remembering: When we let go of the pressure to be exceptional, we create space to learn, adapt, and thrive.

Closer to home, I've often observed my own family—not the best in their fields, not vying for accolades, but deeply happy. Their lives are rooted in the present, finding joy in everyday moments: sharing meals, helping a neighbor, or simply enjoying the rain. They're proof that contentment doesn't come from seeking greatness but from cherishing what you already have. These so-called "average" lives are anything but ordinary; they're rich with meaning and love.

"A successful person is an average person who is focused," said Harvey Mackay. This sentiment beautifully encapsulates the idea that "average" isn't a verdict; it's a space of possibility. It's where growth begins, where resilience is nurtured, and where happiness takes root. Average people—the ones who stay grounded while striving for progress—teach us invaluable lessons about balance, humility, and purpose.

Think about it: How often do we overlook the wisdom of those around us because they don't fit the mold of "exceptional"? The parent balancing work and family with unwavering dedication. The colleague who always finds a way to bring optimism to a stressful project. The teacher who's not aiming for awards but focuses on inspiring one student at a time. These individuals embody what it means to lead a fulfilling life, not through grand gestures but through steady, meaningful contributions.

There's also a cultural dimension to this idea. When surveys or studies share findings, they often reference "average" results. Average, in this context, doesn't mean insignificant—it's a reflection of shared experiences, a reminder that most of us are navigating similar challenges and joys. When we embrace this "average" identity, we find solidarity and connection. We're reminded that being part of the collective is its own kind of greatness.

And yet, embracing "average" doesn't mean complacency. As I've said before, "It's okay to be average, but staying average is bad." The goal isn't to remain static but to grow steadily, at your own pace, in ways that align with your values and aspirations. Average is the starting point, not the destination. It's a mindset that encourages progress without the crushing weight of unrealistic expectations.

So the next time you find yourself comparing your journey to someone else's, pause and reflect on what "average" means to you. Is it a source of dissatisfaction, or can it be a springboard for growth?

Look around at the people in your life who inspire you—not because they've achieved the extraordinary, but because they've mastered the art of finding joy in the ordinary.

Their stories remind us that happiness isn't reserved for those at the top; it's available to all of us, right here, in this moment.

Chapter 8

PROCRASTINATION: THE VILLAIN

"I'll just do it later."

Have you ever said these words, fully intending to act on them, only to feel the weight of unfinished tasks creeping up later? Perhaps it was replying to an email, making an appointment, or organizing that ever-growing stack of papers on your desk. In the moment, delaying the task felt harmless—even justified. But as the hours turned into days, a subtle sense of unease began to settle in. What started as a simple delay became a lingering thought, quietly demanding attention and draining your peace of mind.

Procrastination often disguises itself as a small indulgence. "Take a break," it whispers, "you deserve it." And while there's truth in allowing yourself rest, procrastination has a way of stealing more than just time. It creeps into our routines, builds pressure, and turns once-manageable tasks into daunting obstacles.

As Edward Young so aptly put it, "Procrastination is the thief of time." But this thief doesn't stop at stealing hours from your day. It takes away opportunities for growth, fulfillment, and ultimately, happiness. Procrastination is like a poison that seems sweet at first but turns harmful the longer you let it linger.

One of the greatest challenges with procrastination is that many of us don't even recognize when we're doing it. Even when we do, we often fail to take action. A task gets labeled as "boring" or "unimportant," and so it's pushed aside with a promise to handle it later. And while that promise feels harmless in the moment, the cumulative impact is far from trivial. Unfinished work builds anxiety, creates mental clutter, and chips away at our satisfaction, robbing us of the happiness that comes from feeling accomplished and in control.

Research shows that procrastination is more common than we might think. Around 20% of adults are chronic procrastinators, and another 42–43% admit to procrastinating frequently. Only about 15% claim they rarely procrastinate. Whether it's habitual, the result of misplaced priorities, or driven by fear and self-doubt, procrastination touches nearly everyone in some way.

I remember a moment from my own life when procrastination taught me this lesson the hard way. A small work assignment—something that would have taken me 20 minutes to complete—kept getting pushed back. "Tomorrow is fine," I'd tell myself. But when tomorrow arrived, the task remained untouched. By the end of the week, what was once a minor responsibility had snowballed into a stressful, last-minute scramble. The satisfaction of a job well done was replaced with regret and frustration, all because I had let procrastination take the wheel.

This is the insidious nature of procrastination.

It offers temporary relief while quietly building long-term stress. Often, it's rooted in habits like a lack of self-control, misplaced priorities, or the simple assumption that a task won't significantly impact our lives. Yet the consequences are anything but insignificant. Whether it's delaying journaling, avoiding a difficult conversation, or putting off learning something new, procrastination has a way of undermining even the practices meant to support our growth and happiness.

The reasons behind procrastination are varied. Fear is a common culprit—fear of failure, fear of imperfection. For some, it's boredom or the belief that the task isn't urgent. Others struggle with self-deception, convincing themselves that the delay is justified or harmless.

Procrastination is the sneaky villain in our lives, stealing our peace of mind and holding us back from reaching our potential. It lures us in with the promise of short-term relief, only to trap us in a cycle of regret and stress that drains our well-being.

But here's the good news: once we understand its tricks, we can outsmart it. Whether it's learning to prioritize, cultivating self-awareness, or breaking tasks into manageable steps, overcoming procrastination is entirely possible.

Take back your time, your energy, and your happiness with purposeful action—it's time to show procrastination who's boss.

Understanding Procrastination

Why do we procrastinate?

It's a simple question with complex answers. Procrastination is more than delaying tasks; it's often a symptom of deeper psychological factors. Have you ever told yourself, "I'll do it later," only to feel regret as the deadline loomed closer? You're not alone. The reasons behind procrastination are as varied as the tasks we avoid.

Some of the most common culprits include fear, perfectionism, lack of discipline, and even boredom. Fear can take many forms—fear of failure, fear of criticism, or fear of not meeting expectations. Perfectionism convinces us that unless a task can be done flawlessly, it's not worth starting. Boredom, on the other hand, drains motivation, making even simple tasks feel like insurmountable hurdles. And then there's self-deception: the sly voice in your head that says, "I have time. Tomorrow will be better."

But procrastination isn't laziness. In fact, it often has little to do with a lack of effort. At its core, procrastination stems from emotional avoidance. When a task feels overwhelming or uncomfortable, delaying it seems like a way to avoid those feelings—but only temporarily. The weight of unfinished work doesn't disappear; it lingers, creating mental clutter and anxiety by amplifying triggers like fear of failure, perfectionism, and self-deception. These triggers intertwine to create a vicious cycle, leaving you stuck and stressed.

Do you relate to any of these?

- **Fear of Not Meeting Expectations**: The pressure to succeed can paralyze you. Instead of taking the first step, you hesitate, worried you'll fall short of perfection.

- **Perfectionism**: Tasks feel so monumental that starting them seems impossible. The desire for flawless execution becomes a barrier to progress.

- **Self-Deception**: You convince yourself that delay is harmless. "There's plenty of time," you say, pushing the task aside, only to regret it later.

- **Lack of Vision**: When you don't see the importance of a task, it's easy to dismiss it as unimportant. But these small dismissals accumulate, creating unnecessary stress.

- **Habits and Attitudes**: Often, you procrastinate out of routine. If delaying tasks becomes a habit, breaking the cycle feels daunting.

Understanding these triggers helps us recognize that procrastination isn't about laziness but emotional and psychological barriers that need addressing.

Procrastination doesn't just steal time—it takes a toll on your emotional well-being. Think back to a time when you postponed something important. Did it free you from stress, or did it add a layer of unease as the deadline crept closer?

Unfinished tasks create mental clutter. They occupy space in your mind, distracting you from the present and preventing you from enjoying your day. This mental clutter often leads to self-doubt. You begin questioning your capabilities, which in turn fuels more procrastination. The cycle continues: delay, regret, stress, repeat.

Regret is perhaps one of the most significant impacts of procrastination. How many times have you thought, "This should have been done earlier" or "I should've handled this before"? These thoughts don't just linger; they chip away at your confidence and satisfaction.

The effects of procrastination aren't confined to one area of life—they ripple through your work, relationships, and personal well-being. Imagine putting off a simple task like sending a two-minute acknowledgment email. In the moment, it feels inconsequential. But as days pass, the delay creates a pile-up of small, unfinished tasks. Suddenly, you're facing a backlog that feels unmanageable.

Procrastination not only adds to your workload but also increases the pressure to perform under tighter deadlines.

Unfinished tasks create a sense of incompleteness that occupies your mind. You might find yourself replaying thoughts like, "Why didn't I handle this sooner?" This constant mental chatter prevents you from focusing on other priorities, leaving you feeling overwhelmed.

Procrastination can also strain relationships. Delaying important conversations or responsibilities can lead to misunderstandings and broken trust. For instance, promising to help a loved one but continually postponing it creates tension and feelings of neglect.

I remember a conversation with a colleague who once struggled to keep up with her work schedule. Initially, her procrastination seemed harmless. She'd push minor tasks to the next day, telling herself they weren't urgent. But as these small delays added up, they began to affect her performance. By the time she realized the extent of the issue, her stress levels had skyrocketed.

"It's not that I didn't care," she told me. "I just kept telling myself there was time. But eventually, I felt buried under the weight of everything

I hadn't done." Her experience is a reminder that procrastination isn't about neglecting responsibilities; it's about underestimating the impact of delay.

Swami Vivekananda's words capture the essence of procrastination: "Everything is easy when you are busy. But nothing is easy when you are lazy." While procrastination doesn't equate to laziness, it thrives in moments when we lack readiness or focus.

The antidote? Action.

Even the smallest step forward can break the cycle and restore momentum.

Breaking the Stress Cycle

Procrastination doesn't just delay tasks—it sets off a ripple effect that seeps into every corner of life. When left unchecked, it becomes a self-perpetuating cycle: delay creates stress, stress breeds unhappiness, and unhappiness leads to more delay. Breaking this cycle requires recognizing how procrastination manifests in real-life scenarios and understanding its cascading consequences. Let me take you through a couple of relatable examples that illustrate this.

Do you remember the bike solo trip I shared earlier? Let's revisit that story, because it led to an unexpected lesson about procrastination and its costs. After leaving the minimalist uncle's house, I was making my way toward the hills, enjoying the crisp morning air after a rain-soaked night. Everything seemed perfect until my bike's tire gave out. Luckily, I managed to roll downhill to a garage for repairs. While waiting, I struck up a conversation with another rider who had also stopped for a break. We connected over our shared love for riding, and he kindly invited me to his home for a quick snack—a detour I gladly accepted.

His house was impressive, clearly recently renovated. I couldn't help but compliment him on how beautiful it looked. He smiled, but his expression held a hint of regret. "Thank you," he said, "but this renovation cost me far more than it should have." Intrigued, I asked him to elaborate. His story offers a vivid illustration of how procrastination can spiral into stress and unhappiness.

Here's how he broke it down:

- **The Scenario:** For months, he had delayed minor home repairs—a leaky pipe and some faulty wiring. "It's just a small issue," he thought. A plumber's visit would have cost only ₹500, and the electrical work around ₹2000. Yet, he repeatedly postponed calling a professional, assuring his family that he'd handle it later.

- **The Stress:** Over time, the problems worsened. The leaky pipe began dripping more persistently, and the faulty wiring became a daily concern. His family grew increasingly frustrated, reminding him constantly to get the repairs done. These reminders, meant to nudge him into action, only added to his stress. He began avoiding the conversations altogether, feeling cornered by his own inaction. Trust between him and his family started to fray as they questioned his reliability.

- **The Unhappiness:** One morning, disaster struck. The leaking water came into contact with the faulty wiring, causing a small electrical fire. Fortunately, no one was hurt, but the damage was extensive. What could have been resolved with a few thousand rupees now required a full-scale renovation, costing several lakhs. The financial burden, coupled with the "I told you so" comments from his family, left him feeling overwhelmed and dejected. "I could have saved myself so much trouble," he admitted, "if only I had acted sooner."

As we shared a laugh over his hard-learned lesson, he told me how he finally overcame his procrastination. By creating a simple plan and tackling one task at a time, he managed to stay on top of his responsibilities. "It's not perfect," he said, "but it's better than the stress I used to carry."

This story stayed with me as I continued my journey. It reminded me of another conversation I had with a colleague who faced a similar pattern—but in a professional setting.

She often joked about her tendency to delay tasks, brushing it off as "no big deal." At first, it seemed harmless. She'd push small tasks, like replying to emails or submitting reports, to the next day, thinking they wouldn't make much difference. But as the weeks went on, those small delays began piling up. Here's how her experience unfolded:

- **The Scenario:** Her daily schedule became increasingly chaotic. Emails went unanswered, reports were submitted late, and she started forgetting commitments. Simple tasks that could have been handled in five or ten minutes were repeatedly postponed. Frequent tea breaks and prolonged lunch hours added to the delays. "I'll send this email after lunch," she'd say. "I'll look at that file after a quick game of pool." These small postponements snowballed into a mountain of unfinished work.

- **The Stress:** As her tasks piled up, so did her stress. She began feeling overwhelmed by the sheer volume of work she had to catch up on. Missed deadlines and poor planning led to strained relationships with colleagues, who started seeing her as unreliable. "I felt like I was constantly playing catch-up," she confided. The stress affected her confidence, making her question her capabilities.

- **The Unhappiness:** The cumulative effect of her procrastination was personal dissatisfaction. She no longer found joy in her work, feeling burdened by the tasks she once enjoyed. Her performance reviews reflected the impact, labeling her an "average performer." This label weighed heavily on her, amplifying her unhappiness and further eroding her motivation.

After we spoke, she decided to take charge of her habits. Together, we created a plan that prioritized her tasks and set achievable daily goals. Slowly but surely, she began to rebuild her confidence and found happiness in her work again.

These stories highlight a common thread: procrastination may start small, but its impact can ripple through every aspect of life. It turns manageable tasks into overwhelming burdens, creating stress that affects not just your productivity but also your relationships and sense of self-worth.

So, what was this plan that turned things around for them?

Let's explore how to tackle procrastination head-on and break free from its grip.

Simple Solutions

What if overcoming procrastination wasn't about making massive changes but small, consistent ones?

Breaking the habit doesn't require grand gestures; it starts with self-awareness and a willingness to take one small step at a time. The following strategies can help you regain control and build momentum, even if procrastination feels deeply ingrained.

- **SMART Goals:** Have you ever looked at a large task and felt paralyzed by its size? Breaking it into smaller, actionable steps can make all the difference. SMART stands for Specific, Measurable, Achievable, Relevant, and Time-bound. For example, if your goal is to write a report, start by setting specific tasks like researching for two hours, outlining the structure, and drafting one section per day. Assign deadlines to each part, ensuring they are realistic and align with your overall timeline. By focusing on smaller, measurable steps, you can track progress and feel a sense of accomplishment with each milestone, keeping your motivation high.

- **The Two-Minute Rule:** Some tasks are so small they take less time to complete than to put off. This is where the two-minute rule comes in handy: if a task can be done in two minutes or less, do it immediately. Sending a quick email, tidying your desk, or jotting down a note can be completed in moments, clearing mental space and preventing these small tasks from piling up. The act of finishing even the simplest task builds momentum, making it easier to tackle larger ones.

- **Time-Blocking:** Many of us underestimate the power of focused time. The Pomodoro technique—25 minutes of work followed by a five-minute break—is a simple yet effective method to boost productivity. By blocking specific hours for tasks and treating them as non-negotiable, you create a structure that minimizes distractions. Imagine dedicating 25 minutes to sorting emails or working on a presentation, knowing that a break awaits you. This balance of focus and rest keeps your energy levels steady and your mind clear.

- **To-Do Lists with Priorities:** A to-do list can be a lifesaver—if used effectively. Start each day by listing your tasks and marking the top three priorities. By focusing on high-impact tasks first, you'll gain a sense of accomplishment that motivates you to tackle the rest. Pair this with a reward system: allow yourself a small treat, like a cup of tea or a walk, after completing a priority task. Positive reinforcement makes the process enjoyable and encourages consistency.

- **Self-Awareness Practices:** Understanding why you procrastinate is key to overcoming it. Take a moment to reflect on your triggers. Are you avoiding a task because it feels overwhelming? Or is it because you're afraid of not meeting expectations? Journaling about the tasks you delay and the emotions tied to them can provide valuable insights. Once you identify the root cause, you can address it directly, whether by seeking support, breaking the task into smaller steps, or simply giving yourself permission to start imperfectly.

Overcoming procrastination isn't about perfection; it's about progress.

Each small action you take brings you closer to breaking the cycle and reclaiming your time, energy, and happiness. The journey might feel gradual, but with consistent effort, these solutions can transform procrastination from a habit into a choice.

And that choice? It's entirely within your power.

Reinforcing Positive Habits

Do you remember how good it felt as a child to earn a gold star at school?

That little sticker wasn't just an acknowledgment; it was a motivator. The next day, you'd try harder, eager to experience that same sense of pride and accomplishment.

So why not carry this concept into adulthood? Rewarding yourself for small wins can be a powerful way to maintain motivation and reinforce positive habits.

Celebrating progress doesn't have to be elaborate. It could be something as simple as taking a coffee break, enjoying your favorite snack, or indulging in an hour of guilt-free relaxation after completing a challenging task. These small rewards create a positive association with productivity, making it easier to stay consistent. Imagine finishing a tedious report and treating yourself to a movie night or preparing your favorite meal. These moments of recognition are more than indulgences—they're reinforcements that encourage continued effort.

Visual reminders can also play a significant role in keeping you focused. Write down your goals on sticky notes or use a vision board to keep them in sight. For instance, place a note on your desk that reads, "What can I finish in two minutes right now?" This constant nudge keeps you aligned with your objectives and prevents procrastination from creeping in. Some people find success by setting reminders on their phones or creating colorful to-do lists that turn planning into a fun activity.

Another effective technique is habit pairing—combining a task with an enjoyable activity. For example, listen to your favorite playlist while organizing your workspace or pair making your bed with brewing your morning coffee. These pairings transform mundane tasks into moments of satisfaction, building a routine that's both productive and enjoyable. Consider matching tasks like folding laundry with catching up on your favorite podcast, turning a chore into an anticipated part of your day.

Accountability can also be a game-changer. Share your goals with a trusted friend or colleague who can encourage you and celebrate your progress. For instance, set up a weekly check-in where you both discuss your achievements and challenges. Knowing someone is cheering you on makes the journey less daunting and far more rewarding. This could also mean joining a community group or online forum where members share goals and support each other's progress, fostering a sense of connection and shared purpose.

Mindset matters, too. Shift your perspective from "I have to do this" to "I get to do this."

Framing tasks as opportunities for growth rather than burdens changes how you approach them. Instead of dreading a project, see it as a chance to learn, grow, or make an impact. This small mental shift can transform even the most tedious task into an avenue for personal growth. For example, rather than resenting a lengthy commute, use that time to listen to audiobooks or brainstorm creative ideas.

Incorporating self-talk can also reinforce your efforts. Acknowledge your progress with statements like, "I'm proud of how far I've come today" or "Completing this brings me closer to my bigger goals." Self-encouragement builds resilience and helps counter negative thoughts that fuel procrastination. Paired with a gratitude journal or evening reflection, these practices deepen your sense of accomplishment and keep you focused on the positives.

When you develop these habits, you don't just avoid procrastination—you create a life where productivity feels natural and rewarding.

Each small win reinforces your ability to take charge, creating a ripple effect that touches every aspect of your life. Think of this as crafting a framework for success where each day builds upon the last, creating a foundation of confidence and momentum.

When you celebrate your progress—big or small—you're not just checking off tasks; you're shaping the person you're becoming.

And that person?

They're happier, more confident, and fully in control of their journey.

Remember, procrastination isn't a permanent villain—it's a challenge you can overcome, one task at a time. By breaking free from its grip, you're not merely clearing your schedule; you're opening up space for the relationships, passions, and experiences that truly matter.

Chapter 9

HUMAN BEING IS A SOCIAL ANIMAL

From the moment we are born, our instinct is to reach out. A baby cries for its caregiver, a child grasps their friend's hand as they explore the playground, and as adults, we continue to seek these connections in ways both small and profound. Think of the morning nod exchanged with your neighbor, the warmth of a casual chat over coffee, or the reassurance of a long phone call with someone who knows you well. These moments aren't routine—they ground us, reminding us that we're valued, heard, and part of something larger than ourselves.

Socializing isn't simply having fun; it's finding belonging. Think of the last time you shared a laugh with someone—the warmth it brought, the weight it lifted, even if only for a moment. That's the quiet magic of connection: it lightens our burdens and reminds us we're not alone. Yet, in today's hyper-connected world, where we can reach anyone, anywhere, with the tap of a button, the quality of these interactions has often taken a backseat to their quantity.

The Role of Socializing

Socializing is more than an activity; it's an essential foundation for well-being.

Healthy relationships don't only make life more enjoyable—they actively enhance it. Studies have consistently shown that people with strong social connections tend to live longer, healthier lives. They report higher levels of happiness and are better equipped to handle stress. Socializing is like an invisible thread, creating a sense of belonging and safety that supports us through life's ups and downs.

Looking back at my grandfather's generation, it's amazing how naturally they built connections without any of the tools we cling to today. No smartphones, no social media, no Zoom calls—yet their networks were strong and unwavering. Their secret? Real, in-the-moment interactions. Bonds grew in parks, at local markets, during casual gatherings, or with the unplanned simplicity of dropping by a neighbor's house. Connection wasn't penciled into a calendar; it was part of life's everyday routine.

Fast forward to today. Technology has erased the physical barriers to connection. You can chat with someone across the globe in real-time or reconnect with a childhood friend through a social media app. And while this access is incredible, it can also be overwhelming. Endless friend requests, group chats, and virtual meetings often leave us feeling more drained than fulfilled.

The secret lies not in how many connections we have but in their depth and authenticity.

The benefits of meaningful socializing are undeniable. It boosts our mood, builds our confidence, and fosters self-awareness through the feedback and validation we receive from others. Socializing also reduces stress—those moments of laughter or shared understanding act as a balm for the pressures of daily life. Picture the colleague who made your Monday morning lighter with a joke or the friend who lent an empathetic ear when you needed it most. These interactions don't just fill our days; they fill our hearts.

But like anything, socializing requires balance.

Not every interaction will uplift you. Gossip, negativity, or superficial relationships can sap your energy instead of replenishing it. Being intentional about your social circle is vital. Surround yourself with people who inspire you, who listen without judgment, and who support your growth. This isn't about amassing hundreds of acquaintances; it's about nurturing a handful of deep, meaningful bonds.

The COVID-19 pandemic was a powerful reminder of how deeply human beings value connection, even in the face of immense challenges. During a time of physical distancing, people found creative ways to bridge the gaps—virtual game nights brought laughter into homes, online communities became sanctuaries for shared experiences, and drive-by celebrations allowed milestones to be marked with joy and solidarity. These innovations were not just practical solutions; they symbolized the resilience of human bonds, proving that connection isn't bound by physical closeness but by the effort and care we invest in maintaining it.

Take a moment to reflect on your own social circle.

Are your interactions energizing and uplifting, or do they leave you feeling drained? Are you prioritizing quality over quantity? In the end, it's not the number of connections that defines their value but the depth and authenticity they bring to your life.

Healthy relationships aren't a matter of chance; they're cultivated through care, effort, and genuine intention. When nurtured, these connections can elevate your well-being, bringing a sense of joy and support like nothing else.

So, how can you actively cultivate and sustain these meaningful relationships to create an even brighter, more fulfilling life?

Positive Networks and Support

Do you remember a moment in your life when everything felt like too much to handle and spiraling out of your control?

We've all been there. Perhaps it was a demanding job, the pressure of meeting deadlines, or a personal challenge that left you feeling stuck.

You might remember juggling countless responsibilities, wondering how to move forward, and questioning whether you were enough.

And then, out of the blue, almost like a miracle you didn't even know you needed, someone reached out.

Maybe it was a trusted friend who lent an empathetic ear, a parent who offered advice without knowing how much it meant to you, or a community that welcomed you into its fold with open arms. That connection, however small it seemed at the time, shifted the tide. It lightened the burden, restored your clarity, and reminded you of your resilience.

These moments of connection are transformative. They don't merely reduce stress; they rebuild your self-belief, renew your focus, and reignite your motivation to face whatever comes next.

The power of supportive connections lies in their ability to transform challenges into opportunities.

Casual conversations with neighbors or friendly banter during a morning walk can brighten your day. But intentional networks—whether it's a close-knit circle of friends or a professional community—go a step further. These spaces allow you to share your struggles and triumphs, knowing that the people around you genuinely care about your growth and well-being.

Let me share a story. At a local technology gathering, I met someone who had been struggling with setbacks at work. They felt trapped, overwhelmed by their limitations, and seriously considered leaving their job altogether. During one of these gatherings, they opened up about their challenges. Instead of judgment, they received empathy and actionable advice. Encouraged by the support, they began to view their struggles differently. With time, they regained their confidence, redefined their goals, and even started mentoring others who faced similar hurdles. What began as a moment of vulnerability grew into a transformative experience that improved not just their career but their entire outlook on life.

Building positive networks isn't limited to professional spaces. Think of the friend who calls to check on you after a tough week or the family member who shows up with a home-cooked meal when you're unwell. These connections become pillars of strength, offering a lifeline during difficult times and amplifying joy during moments of celebration. They remind you that you're never truly alone in life's challenges.

Intentional socializing creates resilience.

When you're surrounded by people who uplift you, obstacles feel less intimidating, and setbacks transform into stepping stones. It's about finding balance—seeking help when you need it and offering support in return. This cycle of mutual care strengthens everyone involved, creating an ecosystem of trust and positivity.

Think about the communities you're part of—a local book club where stories spark inspiration, a laughing club where joy becomes contagious, or even a virtual group dedicated to a shared passion. These spaces are more than social gatherings; they're sanctuaries of connection and renewal. They remind you that shared experiences—whether a heartfelt conversation or a collective laugh—are among life's most cherished gifts.

So, how do you build and nurture these networks?

Start by showing up. Be present and genuinely engaged with those around you. Listen deeply to understand, not just to respond. Share your own experiences with honesty and openness. Seek out spaces that prioritize positivity and growth—whether it's a professional forum, a hobby group, or a simple coffee catch-up with a friend. And remember, nurturing a connection isn't about grand gestures. It's the small, consistent acts of care and attention that build trust and deepen bonds over time.

The strength of a network isn't measured by its size but by the quality of trust, empathy, and understanding that flows within it. By focusing on intentional and meaningful relationships, you create a foundation that supports and uplifts you through every phase of life. And yet, in today's world, these connections are often filtered through screens and algorithms.

Social Media and Mental Health

How many hours did you spend on social media yesterday?

Was it a quick scroll during lunch, or did you lose track of time hopping between posts, reels, and stories? Now ask yourself this: How much of that time made you feel genuinely connected or fulfilled?

For many of us, the answers don't align the way we'd hope.

Social media, for all its conveniences, is a double-edged sword. On one hand, it keeps us connected with loved ones, offers windows into new communities, and even helps us discover hobbies or passions. But on the other, it can subtly seep into our mental space, leaving us anxious, dissatisfied, and often more isolated than before.

Let me take you back to a moment from one of my road trips—the same one that's been a thread through so many stories so far. I had stopped at a small, quiet bookstall on a serene street lined with vendors and the occasional honk of passing scooters. The faint aroma of chai wafted from a nearby tea stall, mingling with the soft hum of conversations around me. As I browsed through the shelves, my fingers landed on a book just as someone else reached for the same title. We exchanged a smile, and that small moment sparked a conversation.

He introduced himself as a counselor who worked with people struggling with stress, and as we talked, he shared an insight that struck a chord: "More than 60% of the people I work with don't even realize how much they're abusing social media." He spoke of how endless scrolling, curated comparisons, and the lure of digital validation can silently chip away at mental well-being. "People know they should take breaks, reduce screen time—but how many actually follow through?" he asked, his tone equal parts curious and concerned. It wasn't a lecture; it felt like an invitation to reflect.

As he spoke, I thought of how often we turn to social media for connection, only to walk away feeling hollow. A friend's vacation photos might spark envy. A colleague's success story might make us question our own path. What starts as a way to stay connected can sometimes magnify insecurities we didn't even know we had.

Think about your own experiences. Have you ever logged onto a social platform to feel closer to friends or family, only to find yourself spiraling into comparison? Someone else's promotion, vacation pictures, or curated snippets of "perfect" moments can leave you questioning your own journey. Social media has the power to connect, but it can also amplify insecurities if not approached mindfully.

But let's not dismiss it entirely.

When used with intention, social media can be a source of joy and connection. It's where you can nurture bonds with loved ones across distances and discover communities that resonate with your passions—be it Indian classical dance, regional cooking, or gardening. During the pandemic, many people used these platforms to create content, share knowledge, and even build livelihoods. For some, it became a lifeline in isolating times. This duality—connection versus comparison—defines the nuanced role of social media in our lives.

So, how do you strike the right balance? Start with awareness. Pay attention to how social media makes you feel.

Are you logging off feeling inspired and connected, or does it leave you restless and drained?

Setting boundaries can help. For instance, designate specific times during the day to check your accounts and avoid endless scrolling. Turn off notifications to prevent being lured back into the digital vortex every few minutes.

Be selective about the content you consume.

Follow accounts and pages that uplift, educate, or inspire rather than provoke envy or dissatisfaction. The counselor I met suggested a "digital cleanse" routine: periodically unfollowing accounts that don't add value to your mental and emotional well-being. Replace passive scrolling with active engagement. Commenting on a friend's post or sharing something meaningful can foster real connections rather than superficial interactions.

And most importantly, balance your online interactions with offline moments.

Schedule time for face-to-face conversations, whether it's catching up with a friend over chai or taking a walk with a neighbor. These moments anchor you in the present and nurture deeper, more authentic connections.

During the pandemic, we witnessed the potential of digital platforms to unite and inspire. But we also saw how excessive screen time led to burnout and a sense of disconnection. The key is to find balance—using social media to support, not replace, real-life relationships.

In a world increasingly dominated by screens, it's easy to overlook the warmth of a shared laugh or the comfort of a genuine conversation. But as you navigate this digital age, pause, reflect, and prioritize connections that truly matter.

After all, these are the lasting, meaningful relationships that stand strong in an ever-changing world.

Keeping up with Genuine Bonds

Humans are, by nature, social beings. Yet, in the rush of daily life, it's easy to let relationships slip into the background—to tell yourself you'll call that old friend "tomorrow" or visit a relative "next month." And before you know it, weeks turn into months, and those meaningful connections start to slip away. But when you pause and reflect, it's often these genuine bonds that carry you through life's ups and downs.

Think back to a time when life felt particularly heavy—a career setback that tested your confidence, a health scare that disrupted your rhythm, or a phase of loneliness that seemed endless.

Who were the people who stood by you?

Chances are, it wasn't the sea of names on your social media feed; it was likely the aunt who called to check in, the neighbor who brought over a warm bowl of dal during a tough time, or the childhood friend who made you laugh at your lowest. In moments like these, the strength of meaningful relationships shines—a strength built on trust, empathy, and a shared history of showing up for one another.

In India, connections often go beyond the immediate family. It's the uncle from your building who always stops for a quick chat, the shopkeeper who remembers your preferences, or the friends who turn into extended family. These bonds are woven into our everyday lives, offering a sense of belonging that uplifts even the hardest days. It's a reminder that meaningful relationships aren't measured by how many people you know, but by how deeply you connect with those around you.

So take that first step. Invite a friend over for chai or knock on your neighbor's door to share a small moment of conversation. Imagine the warmth of sitting together, laughing over life's quirks, or the reassurance of knowing someone is truly listening. A simple 15-minute exchange can brighten your day in ways you never anticipated. As you reach out, be fully present. Set your phone aside, meet their eyes, and listen with genuine intent.

You don't have to say all the right things; you just have to offer your time, your attention, and your heart.

Shared activities can also strengthen bonds in ways that words alone cannot. Join a yoga class with a friend, cook a meal together, or revive an old family tradition like Sunday lunches. These moments create memories and reinforce the sense of belonging that's so integral to happiness. For instance, a weekly cricket game with neighbors or a simple walk in the park with your sibling can leave you feeling lighter and more connected.

Celebrating milestones—whether big or small—is another way to nurture relationships. Acknowledge a colleague's promotion, surprise a friend on their birthday, or simply express gratitude for someone's presence in your life. These acts of recognition, though seemingly small, carry immense emotional weight. It's these moments of thoughtfulness that deepen the connections we hold dear.

Conflict, too, is a natural part of any relationship. Avoiding it doesn't strengthen bonds; addressing it does. Approach disagreements with empathy, seeking to understand the other person's perspective rather than simply defending your own. When handled with care, conflicts can become opportunities to deepen trust and mutual respect. Imagine how addressing a misunderstanding with a friend can transform tension into a stronger, more resilient connection.

During the pandemic, many families rediscovered the joy of shared traditions. Some began having regular video calls, others cooked meals together, even if it was over Zoom. My own family has a tradition of coming together—whether it's to celebrate a milestone or simply to support one another during a challenging time. Even something as simple as sharing updates in a family group chat brought comfort and a sense of unity. We've kept this alive, even when physical distance separates us. It's not the scale of the gesture that matters but the consistency and intention behind it.

To keep these bonds strong, invest in shared experiences. Visit an old school friend for tea, join a community club, or participate in a local festival. These collective moments remind us of the joy found in togetherness, a joy that grows richer with time.

Genuine bonds are built on a foundation of trust, respect, and shared moments. They don't demand grand gestures but thrive on the small, everyday acts of care and connection. And while building these relationships takes effort, the rewards—a sense of belonging, support, and shared joy—are immeasurable.

In the end, it's not about how many people you know but how deeply you connect with those who truly matter. The richness of life lies not in the breadth of your network but in the depth of your relationships.

And as we look inward, toward cultivating a fulfilling inner life, we'll discover how these external connections become even more meaningful.

Chapter 10

'MIRROR, MIRROR': FINDING HAPPINESS WITHIN YOURSELF

"Objects in the mirror are closer than they appear."

Ever noticed that little line on your car's side mirror? We see it all the time, but have you ever stopped to think about what it really means? Sure, it's there to warn drivers, but it's also a reminder about life. The person staring back at you in the mirror—that's the person who knows you best. Your thoughts, fears, dreams—no one understands them better than you. It's a powerful thought, isn't it?

As the first light of day filters through the curtains, you stand in front of the mirror. The house is still, the noise of the day hasn't yet begun. You lean in closer, studying your reflection—not just the surface details like a stray hair or the shadows beneath your eyes, but the person looking back at you. Who are they? Are they someone you're proud of? Someone you trust?

It's a small, everyday act, glancing in the mirror, but what if it became more than routine? What if, in that moment, you chose to truly see yourself—not through the lens of others' opinions or the comparisons we so often make—but as you are, with all your strengths, flaws, and potential?

This is where happiness begins.

Not in the validation of the world, but in the quiet realization that the only person who truly holds the key to your joy is staring right back at you. The mirror doesn't lie; it reflects the person who has the power to change, to grow, and to find fulfillment.

You know it's true when they say happiness doesn't come from outside—it's not something someone else can hand to you. It's something you build within yourself, step by step, by taking responsibility and working on self-improvement. Real growth happens not by competing with others, but by being honest with yourself.

You already know this deep down—now it's time to act on it.

As you look into the mirror tomorrow morning, ask yourself this: "Am I living a life that fulfills me? Am I taking steps to be the person I want to be?" These aren't questions to avoid or delay, but ones that can guide you toward clarity and purpose.

So how do we move from this moment of reflection to meaningful action? How do we transform self-awareness into growth? It starts by understanding that healthy competition begins with yourself.

The Concept of Healthy Competition

Think of a cricket player at the end of a match. The stadium lights dim, the cheers fade, and the scoreboard is reset. What remains is the player, quietly reviewing the game in their mind—each swing of the bat, each missed opportunity. They aren't focused on how others played; they're dissecting their own performance, searching for ways to improve. That's the essence of healthy competition: not measuring yourself against others, but striving to outdo your own yesterday.

Now think of your own life.

How often do you fall into the trap of comparing yourself to others? Maybe it's a colleague who seems to achieve everything effortlessly, or a friend whose social media posts paint the perfect life. These comparisons can leave you feeling inadequate, chasing someone else's goals instead of your own. But what if you flipped the script? What if, instead of looking outward, you looked inward? What if the only person you aimed to surpass was the one staring back at you in the mirror?

Competition is a natural part of human behavior. From school exams to job interviews, we're conditioned to compete for recognition, success, and a sense of accomplishment. And while competition can drive us to push boundaries and achieve more, it can also lead to stress, jealousy, and burnout when it's rooted in unhealthy comparisons. When the focus shifts from self-improvement to proving your worth to others, the joy of growth is replaced by the pressure to perform.

Healthy competition begins with shifting your perspective. Instead of seeing others as benchmarks, view them as sources of inspiration. If someone excels in an area where you're struggling, appreciate their strengths and reflect on what you can learn from them. This isn't about ego or envy; it's about growth. Imagine a football team—the players don't focus solely on defeating their opponents. They analyze their own plays, identify areas for improvement, and work collaboratively to become a stronger unit. It's the same in life. Competing with yourself means setting your own goals, learning from your past mistakes, and celebrating progress, no matter how small.

I remember a time when I felt stuck in my career. It seemed like everyone around me was moving ahead, achieving milestones I hadn't even dreamed of yet. The more I compared myself to them, the more defeated I felt. Then, I had a moment of self-awareness—I realized I was measuring my worth against someone else's journey. That realization was a turning point. I decided to focus solely on myself, setting personal benchmarks and tracking my own growth—not anyone else's. The change was transformative. I began to appreciate my journey, becoming more mindful of my strengths and areas for growth. With each small achievement, my confidence grew. That's the power of self-awareness and healthy competition: it shifts your focus from external validation to internal fulfillment.

This mindset is particularly important in professional settings. Offices often breed unhealthy competition, where colleagues vie for recognition at the expense of collaboration. But organizations that cultivate a culture of healthy competition—where growth and accountability are prioritized—create environments where individuals and teams thrive. It's not about being a "family," because workplaces are ultimately driven by goals and outcomes. Instead, it's about cultivating a growth-oriented culture where feedback is constructive, goals are clear, and achievements are celebrated collectively. Imagine a workplace where people uplift each other, where the success of one person is viewed as a win for the whole team. That's the result of healthy competition.

Healthy competition also fuels creativity and innovation. When you're focused on bettering yourself, you're more likely to think outside the box, adapt to challenges, and embrace change. It's no longer about avoiding failure but learning from it. Athletes do this all the time. After every game, they review their performance—not to dwell on mistakes but to use them as stepping stones for growth. This approach applies to all aspects of life. Whether it's a hobby, a relationship, or a career goal, striving to be better than you were yesterday unlocks potential you didn't know you had.

So how can you apply healthy competition to your own life?

Start by identifying areas where you want to grow. Maybe it's improving your fitness, enhancing your skills at work, or deepening your relationships. Set specific, achievable goals and track your progress regularly. Instead of comparing your journey to someone else's, measure your growth against your own past performance. Celebrate your wins— big or small—and use setbacks as opportunities to learn and adapt.

Healthy competition means striving for excellence while showing respect and empathy for yourself and others. It's not focused on being the best in the world; it's focused on becoming the best version of yourself. With this mindset, competition turns into a source of motivation instead of stress, a tool for growth instead of a trigger for insecurity.

As you embrace this perspective, you'll find that the conversations you have with yourself—your self-talk—play a crucial role in sustaining this journey. The voice in your head can either be your harshest critic or your biggest cheerleader.

So, how do you harness the power of self-talk to fuel your growth?

The Power of Self Talk

Do you remember the story of "Snow White and the Seven Dwarfs"? The queen, consumed by vanity and envy, asked her enchanted mirror time and again, "Mirror, mirror on the wall, who is the fairest of them all?" For a while, the mirror's answer fed her ego, bringing satisfaction. But when it reflected a truth she wasn't ready to accept—that someone else was fairer—it shattered her illusion and sent her spiraling into bitterness. The mirror wasn't at fault; it simply held up an unfiltered truth. The queen's downfall lay in her inability to embrace what she saw and grow from it.

Now, imagine your own reflection. Not a magical mirror, but a simple one in your bedroom or bathroom. What would happen if you stood before it and asked yourself a different question? Instead of seeking validation, what if you looked yourself in the eye and asked, "Am I being kind to myself?" or "Am I speaking to myself in a way that builds me up?"

The truth is, self-talk is like that mirror—it reflects what's inside you. And, like the queen, the way you handle that reflection determines whether you grow or remain trapped in negativity.

What is Self-Talk?

Self-talk is the ongoing conversation you have with yourself. It's that inner voice narrating your experiences, guiding your decisions, and influencing your emotions. Sometimes, it's supportive, like a coach cheering you on. Other times, it can be critical, amplifying doubts and fears. Think back to the last time you faced a challenge. Did your inner voice say, "I've got this" or did it whisper, "What if I fail?"

This inner dialogue shapes how you approach life. Positive self-talk can be a tool for resilience and confidence, while negative self-talk often spirals into stress and self-doubt. It's not just words—it's a reflection of how you perceive yourself and your capabilities. The good news? You have the power to change it.

The Impact of Positive Self-Talk

Imagine you're preparing for an important presentation at work. Your heart races as you think of standing in front of your colleagues. Now, your inner voice has two choices. It can say, "You're going to mess this up. They'll see right through you." Or it can say, "You've practiced. You know your material. You're ready for this." Which one do you think sets you up for success?

Positive self-talk is more than a pep talk; it's a mindset. Andre Agassi, the legendary tennis player, famously used self-talk during matches. Unable to receive coaching mid-game, he relied on his inner dialogue to stay focused and motivated. Sometimes, he'd even yell at himself on the court, a visible reminder of the mental battle athletes face. His self-talk wasn't always gentle, but it was constructive—designed to push him forward rather than hold him back.

This principle applies to everyday life too. Whether you're calming your nerves before a job interview, motivating yourself during a workout, or navigating a difficult conversation, the way you speak to yourself matters.

Positive self-talk builds confidence, helps you manage stress, and keeps you grounded in challenging situations.

So, how do you turn your inner critic into a supportive coach? It starts with awareness and intention. Here are some practical ways to cultivate positive self-talk:

- **Start with Affirmations:** Begin your day with simple, affirmative statements. Look in the mirror and say, "I am capable," or "Today is an opportunity to grow." It might feel awkward at first, but over time, these words create new mental patterns.

- **Use a Journal:** At the end of each day, jot down three things you did well and one area you want to improve. Reflecting on your strengths and setting constructive goals helps shift your focus from criticism to growth.

- **Challenge Negative Thoughts:** When a negative thought creeps in, ask yourself, "Is this true? What evidence do I have?" Often, you'll find that your fears are exaggerated, and your capabilities are stronger than you give yourself credit for.

- **Role-Play with Your Mirror Self:** If you're preparing for a big moment, rehearse in front of a mirror. Talk through your fears, your hopes, and your plan. Speak to yourself as you would to a dear friend—with encouragement and empathy.

- **Find Inspiration in Stories:** Shane Koyczan's poignant reminder, "If you can't see anything beautiful about yourself, get a better mirror," highlights the importance of perspective. If you're struggling, surround yourself with uplifting influences—books, podcasts, or even people who remind you of your worth.

Self-talk isn't just about words; it's about creating a mental environment where you can thrive. Positive dialogue fosters empathy, gratitude, and self-compassion. It reminds you to treat yourself with the kindness you readily offer others.

As you begin to shift your inner dialogue, you'll notice something remarkable. The world around you might not change immediately, but your perspective will. Challenges that once felt insurmountable become opportunities to learn. Criticism, instead of shattering your confidence, becomes constructive feedback. And setbacks, rather than defining your journey, become stepping stones toward growth.

Happiness, like self-talk, is an inside job. When you speak to yourself with respect and encouragement, you're not just changing your thoughts; you're reshaping your reality. This is how you build resilience. This is how you nurture confidence. And this is how you make peace with the person staring back at you in the mirror.

When you start strengthening your inner dialogue, something transformative happens—you begin to truly own your journey, free from the weight of comparisons or societal expectations. Step by step, you'll realize that self-talk isn't merely a tool; it's the foundation of living a meaningful and authentic life, shaped by your unique experiences and aspirations.

Embracing Individual Journeys

Take a moment to look at your fingertips. Those intricate patterns—loops, whorls, and arches—are entirely yours. No one else in the world shares your exact fingerprints. Just like these ridges, your life path is unique. Yet how often do we overlook this individuality, caught in the endless loop of comparison? How often do we measure ourselves against someone else's milestones, forgetting that our journey was never meant to mirror theirs?

Your path is unlike any other. Each decision, challenge, and triumph shapes a story that only you can tell. But to fully embrace this narrative, you must first recognize its value. Self-awareness is the key to unlocking this perspective—it allows you to appreciate your strengths and accept your imperfections without judgment. When you see your life as a book in progress, each chapter, with all its twists and turns, becomes a crucial part of the story.

Your journey, like your reflection, like your fingerprint, is one of a kind. Every twist, every triumph, every challenge shapes the story of who you are. Self-awareness is the secret to seeing the bigger picture—it helps you own your strengths while accepting your imperfections, knowing they work together to create your unique, authentic self. Each experience leaves its mark, not as a scar, but as a signature of your growth and resilience.

Self-awareness enables you to view your life objectively. For instance, think of someone learning to play the sitar. Initially, their fingers stumble over the strings, producing uneven notes. But with persistence and practice, those early struggles transform into melodies that resonate. Similarly, your struggles are stepping stones, teaching resilience and patience. When you frame your journey through this lens, comparison loses its power, and your progress becomes the focus.

Everyone you meet has their own story—filled with successes, struggles, and valuable lessons. Instead of envying their achievements, think: What can I learn from their journey? How can their strengths inspire me? With a simple shift in perspective, you can turn comparison into curiosity and envy into motivation.

When you meet someone who excels in areas where you might struggle, see it as an opportunity to learn. For example, a friend's creativity or a colleague's resilience can serve as a reminder of qualities worth cultivating. It's not about mirroring their journey but about enriching your own by embracing new perspectives.

One of my favorite examples is about a close friend who struggled early in their career. Surrounded by peers who seemed to excel effortlessly, they often felt left behind. But instead of giving in to self-doubt, they started observing what made their colleagues stand out. Over time, they identified traits they admired—perseverance, creativity, and adaptability—and worked on building those qualities in themselves. By focusing on their own growth instead of competing with others, they not only advanced in their career but also gained a deeper understanding of their own strengths.

When you look at others' successes as chances to learn instead of threats, something amazing happens. You start seeing the differences in people—not just in backgrounds and experiences but in the unique paths they take—as sources of inspiration. This mindset can help you build stronger connections, show empathy, and genuinely respect others. As you focus on your growth, you'll discover the power of gratitude and care, not as separate actions but as key parts of embracing who you are.

Gratitude can transform your mindset. When you focus on what you have instead of what you're missing, your energy shifts from wanting to appreciating. This doesn't mean you stop aiming higher—it means you recognize and value where you are right now as part of your journey. Practicing gratitude helps you see how far you've come and gives you a chance to celebrate both your wins and the lessons you've learned.

Take inspiration from Indian festivals like Diwali or Pongal. These aren't just celebrations—they're about giving thanks. Whether it's for a good harvest or for hope and renewal, they remind us to appreciate the journey and the milestones along the way. You can do this too. Reflect on what you've achieved, no matter how small, and celebrate those moments.

Self-care is another crucial aspect of honoring your individuality. It's not indulgence; it's sustenance. Whether it's spending quiet moments journaling your thoughts, taking a walk to clear your mind, or engaging in activities that bring you joy, self-care reinforces the idea that your well-being matters. It's a reminder that you're worthy of the time and effort it takes to nurture yourself.

When you fully embrace your unique path, you gain the confidence to face life's challenges with grace. You stop looking sideways, wondering how others are faring, and start looking inward, asking, "What can I learn from this moment? How can I grow from this experience?"

Every journey has its own rhythm. Some days will be filled with breakthroughs; others may test your patience. But as long as you stay true to yourself and honor the journey you're on, you'll find happiness in the process.

As you celebrate your individuality and find strength in your own story, something shifts. Competition no longer feels like a threat—it becomes an opportunity for growth. With this newfound perspective, you'll begin to see the beauty in respecting not just your journey but also those of others. This respect, when paired with gratitude, creates a powerful foundation for healthy competition.

Gratitude in Competition

When you fully embrace your unique path, competition begins to take on a new meaning. It stops being a race to outshine others and becomes a chance to refine your abilities, pushing you closer to your potential. But there's an essential ingredient that transforms competition from a source of stress to a wellspring of growth: gratitude.

Gratitude in competition isn't about diminishing your drive to succeed; it's about recognizing the value of those who challenge you. Think about Sachin Tendulkar, one of cricket's greatest icons. His journey wasn't defined by a need to dominate but by a relentless desire to improve—a desire fueled by the respect he had for his competitors. Even in the face of fierce rivalry, he viewed his opponents not as adversaries to conquer but as contributors to his growth. He often credited his elder brother, Ajit, for analyzing his performances with a critical eye, using each dismissal as a lesson. This approach didn't just make him a better player; it solidified his reputation as a humble yet formidable force in cricket.

Now, think of your own life. Perhaps it's a colleague who consistently excels at presentations or a friend whose discipline inspires admiration. Instead of viewing their achievements through a lens of envy, what if you saw them as opportunities to learn? Gratitude shifts the narrative. Instead of asking, "Why aren't I as good as them?" you begin to ask, "What can I learn from their approach?"

This mindset fosters a growth-oriented approach to competition. Gratitude helps you see setbacks not as failures but as feedback. It encourages you to celebrate others' strengths while honing your own.

I once met a manager at a professional forum who stood out for his empathy and unwavering support. He set an extraordinary example of gratitude in a competitive environment. When his colleague missed a deserved promotion due to an oversight, this manager chose to forgo his own salary increment to ensure fairness. His actions weren't rooted in self-sacrifice alone but in an understanding that shared success fosters collective growth. Such acts of gratitude not only build trust but also create a culture of mutual respect and resilience.

Approaching competition with gratitude helps you stay positive. It doesn't mean losing ambition—it means using it constructively. Gratitude builds resilience, helps you recover from setbacks, and reduces stress by keeping the focus on progress, not perfection.

In team settings, gratitude becomes a powerful force for collaboration. When every member appreciates the strengths of others, rivalries dissolve into partnerships. Picture a workplace where colleagues acknowledge each other's contributions rather than compete for recognition. This environment doesn't just elevate individual performance; it strengthens the entire group. Teams built on gratitude and respect are more adaptable, innovative, and harmonious.

So how can you integrate gratitude into your approach to competition? Start small. At the end of each day, take a moment to reflect on the people who've influenced you, directly or indirectly. Maybe it's a teammate whose dedication raised the bar or a mentor whose feedback reshaped your perspective. Write down these reflections in a journal. Acknowledging these contributions doesn't only benefit your mindset; it strengthens your connections with others.

Another practical step is to vocalize your gratitude. A simple "thank you" can go a long way in recognizing someone's impact. Whether it's an email to a colleague who helped you or a casual conversation with a peer who inspired you, expressing appreciation deepens your relationships and fosters a spirit of encouragement.

Gratitude also helps you build empathy. When you appreciate the challenges others face to achieve their goals, you're more likely to support them rather than compete against them destructively. This perspective shift creates a ripple effect. Just as a small act of kindness can brighten someone's day, a genuine expression of gratitude can transform the dynamics of a competitive environment.

As you adopt this mindset, you'll find that competition becomes less about winning and more about evolving. It's no longer a zero-sum game; it's a shared journey where everyone's progress enriches the collective experience. You'll begin to see rivals as collaborators in disguise, each one playing a role in your growth.

True happiness lies in blending self-growth with respect and gratitude—for yourself and for those who challenge you. By embracing this approach, you'll find that competition doesn't need to be a source of stress or division. Instead, it can be a catalyst for mutual growth, resilience, and fulfillment.

As you cultivate these qualities, you'll notice how self-accountability and external connections work in harmony. They're not opposing forces but complementary paths to a life of meaning, growth, and joy. Each step you take, grounded in gratitude and respect, brings you closer to a version of yourself that not only thrives but also uplifts those around you.

Take a moment to return to where this journey began—the mirror.

Every time you look at your reflection, you're reminded that the person staring back is both your greatest ally and your most profound competitor. This reflection, the essence of *Mirror, Mirror*, holds all your potential, your growth, and your happiness. "Objects in the mirror are closer than they appear," the familiar line reads. And indeed, your dreams, your resilience, and your ability to improve are closer than you often realize. They are within reach, waiting for you to embrace them with gratitude, respect, and self-accountability.

The real competition is never against others. It's the daily commitment to being better than you were yesterday, to honoring your unique path, and to building a life where your reflection becomes a source of pride and peace.

Chapter 11

ACCEPTANCE IS THE KEY TO HAPPINESS

Have you ever missed a bus?

You stand in the sweltering heat as it pulls away, the noise of honking rickshaws and chattering commuters surrounding you. Frustration bubbles up, mixing with the chaos of the busy street. But then, as you wipe the sweat from your brow and glance around, you pause. Life hasn't come to a standstill; another bus will arrive, or perhaps you'll wave down an auto and discover an unexpected conversation along the way.

In that pause, something remarkable happens—acceptance.

You let go of what you can't control and begin to work with what is. That small act of acceptance doesn't just salvage your day; it opens up unexpected possibilities.

Acceptance is often misunderstood. People see it as surrender or defeat, a passive shrug to life's challenges. But true acceptance is far from passive. It's an active choice to acknowledge reality, to work with it instead of resisting it. And in that choice lies a quiet strength—a strength that brings peace, clarity, and the ability to move forward.

The spiritual teacher Eckhart Tolle captured this idea perfectly when he said, "Acceptance looks like a passive state, but in reality, it brings something entirely new into this world. That peace, a subtle energy vibration, is consciousness."

Think about that. Acceptance isn't giving up; it's waking up. It's seeing the world as it is—not as you wish it to be or fear it might become—and responding with clarity and purpose.

Think of missing that bus again. You stood there, helpless, as it pulled away, leaving you in a cloud of dust and disappointment. The day's plans suddenly felt derailed. But then, as the initial frustration passed, you realized something: there's always another way. Maybe it's a rickshaw that will take you on an unexpected shortcut or a quick walk to the metro that clears your mind. That shift, from resisting the loss of control to finding your next step, is acceptance in action. It's not about giving up but about adapting and moving forward despite the setback.

When you practice acceptance, you release the burden of striving against what you can't change. Instead of fighting reality, you learn to flow with it. This isn't easy, of course. It takes mindfulness, patience, and a willingness to let go of the illusion of control. But the rewards are profound. Acceptance brings peace—a kind of peace that isn't tied to external circumstances but rooted in the way you choose to engage with life.

To fully appreciate the power of acceptance, let's start by understanding what it truly means. How does acknowledging reality become the foundation for change and growth? And how can embracing yourself, others, and life's unpredictable situations lead to greater happiness?

Understanding Acceptance

Have you ever been turned down for something you really wanted—a job, a promotion, or even a heartfelt favor? In that moment, rejection can feel like a personal failure, as though the world has conspired to thwart your plans. But if you reflect on such moments, you'll realize they often hold an unexpected lesson. Maybe that job wasn't the right fit, or that setback led you to an opportunity you hadn't considered before. When you pause to accept what happened instead of resisting it, you begin to see the possibilities beyond the disappointment.

Acceptance isn't a passive shrug of defeat; it's an active choice. It's looking at reality without judgment or resistance and saying, "This is what's in front of me. Now, what can I do with it?"

If happiness is a choice, then acceptance is the practice that makes it achievable.

True acceptance starts with understanding—acknowledging reality as it is, not as you wish it to be—and then using that clarity as a foundation for growth.

Why is this so powerful? Because when you practice acceptance, you release the mental and emotional burden of fighting against what you cannot change. Instead of getting stuck in frustration, you allow yourself to focus on what can be done. This shift creates a sense of calm and fosters resilience, equipping you to handle life's uncertainties with grace.

Consider something as mundane as a sudden downpour derailing your plans. You were all set to head out for dinner with friends, but the skies opened up, flooding the roads and trapping you indoors. At first, the frustration bubbles over. But then, acceptance steps in. You realize you can still connect with your friends through a video call or enjoy the evening with a homemade meal. The rain becomes less of a setback and more of a prompt to adapt. This small act of embracing the situation—of working with it rather than against it—is a microcosm of how acceptance shapes our lives.

Acceptance isn't just situational. It's a mindset that permeates every aspect of life. When you embrace reality, you start to notice things you might have overlooked in the haze of resistance. You become more mindful, more aware of the present moment. And with that awareness comes clarity—about what's within your control and what isn't.

This clarity is liberating. It allows you to stop wasting energy on things you can't change and channel it into areas where you can make a difference. Acceptance, then, becomes the foundation for a growth mindset. By acknowledging what is, you create the space to explore what could be. It's not about giving up; it's about letting go of what holds you back so you can move forward.

Take a moment to reflect on your own life. How often do you resist situations, people, or outcomes simply because they don't align with your expectations? How much energy do you spend wishing things were different instead of working with what is? Acceptance invites you to shift that perspective. It asks you to meet reality with curiosity rather than frustration, with openness rather than resistance.

Let's return to that missed bus. In that moment, acceptance isn't resigning yourself to a ruined day. It's simply recognizing that your plans might need to change and finding the best way to adapt. It's about seeing the bigger picture—that one missed bus doesn't define your day, just as one setback doesn't define your life. When you learn to respond this way, you cultivate resilience. And with resilience comes the strength to face challenges head-on, knowing that you'll find a way through.

Understanding acceptance also deepens your connections—with yourself, with others, and with the world around you. It helps you approach people and situations with empathy and patience, recognizing that everyone is navigating their own challenges. This shift fosters stronger relationships and a more balanced, fulfilling life.

Acceptance is the quiet strength that empowers change. It's the inner calm that allows you to face life's storms without losing your footing. When you embrace this practice, you start living in the real world—not the one shaped by your fears or expectations but the one where growth, joy, and peace are possible.

Once we understand acceptance as a foundation for resilience and growth, the next step is to turn this outward gaze inward. How can embracing yourself—your strengths, your flaws, your unique journey—lead to greater happiness?

Self-Acceptance

Ever found yourself lying in bed, wide awake, replaying every little mistake in your head? Tossing, turning, and feeling like your own worst critic? Or standing in front of the mirror, and not liking who you see? That nagging inner voice never seems to let up, always pointing out what you could've done better—no matter how much you've accomplished. Sound familiar? We've all been there, caught in those moments when it feels like nothing is ever quite enough.

For one writer I know, this inner critic was a constant companion. Struggling with a stammer that made even everyday conversations daunting, they avoided speaking up in groups, afraid of being judged. But instead of letting this hold them back, they turned to writing—a medium where their voice flowed freely without hesitation. Through the simple act of embracing what they could do rather than fixating on what they couldn't, they not only found their confidence but also a deeper connection to themselves. That's the transformative power of self-acceptance.

Self-acceptance is key to happiness. It's about acknowledging your strengths and weaknesses without judgment, treating yourself with the same kindness and compassion you would offer a close friend. This doesn't mean ignoring your flaws or refusing to grow—it means starting from a place of understanding and empathy, rather than criticism.

When you accept yourself as you are, you create room for inner peace and personal growth. You stop chasing external validation and begin to value the unique individual staring back at you in the mirror.

Why is self-acceptance so important? Because it sets the stage for a healthier, more fulfilling life. When you accept yourself, you reduce the pressure to meet unrealistic standards set by society or even by your own inner critic. You become more grounded, more mindful, and better equipped to handle life's challenges. Without the constant need to prove yourself, you're free to focus on what truly matters: growing as a person, building meaningful relationships, and pursuing your passions with authenticity.

When you accept yourself, you start comparing yourself less to others and more to your own past self. Intrinsic motivation becomes a habit. You're no longer running a race against everyone else; you're simply striving to be better than you were yesterday. This shift in perspective allows you to define your values and priorities with clarity. Decision-making becomes easier because it's rooted in a deep understanding of who you are and what you stand for.

But how do you practice self-acceptance in a world that constantly pushes us to focus on our shortcomings? Start small. Celebrate your wins, no matter how minor they seem. I have a tradition of gifting myself something meaningful each year I complete in my industry. It's my way of acknowledging my efforts and growth, a reminder that every step forward is worth recognizing. Similarly, you can mark your own milestones with simple acts of self-celebration—a favorite meal, a quiet moment of reflection, or even a handwritten note of gratitude to yourself.

Another vital step is learning to let go of things outside your control. The weather, traffic, or even other people's opinions—these are not battles you need to fight. Instead, focus on what's within your power: your actions, your mindset, and your choices. I once spoke with a friend who, despite being mentally strong, knew his physical limitations. He chose to avoid conflict not out of fear but out of wisdom, redirecting his energy toward solutions rather than unnecessary battles.

Practicing self-love and forgiveness is equally important. As Buddha wisely said, "If your compassion does not include yourself, it is incomplete."

Think about that for a moment. How often do we offer kindness to others but deny it to ourselves? Self-compassion means giving yourself permission to make mistakes, to grow at your own pace, and to forgive yourself for not being perfect. It's about being true to who you are without letting ego or obsession take over. When self-love is balanced with mindfulness, it becomes a force for growth rather than a trap of self-centeredness.

But self-acceptance doesn't happen overnight. It's a journey, one that requires patience and intentionality. But as you begin to embrace yourself—your strengths, your flaws, and everything in between—you'll find a sense of peace that external achievements or validation could never provide. You'll discover that happiness isn't about changing who you are but about appreciating the person you've always been!

When you've rooted yourself in self-acceptance, you're better prepared to face life's unpredictable moments with grace. Situational acceptance—the ability to adapt and thrive in the face of unexpected challenges—becomes not only possible but natural.

It's a reminder that the way you treat yourself shapes the way you handle the world.

Situational Acceptance

Adapting to unexpected changes with a positive mindset can feel challenging, especially when life throws a curveball your way. But acceptance doesn't mean you resign to fate—it's about shifting your focus from what's outside your control to what you can influence. This mindset isn't about giving up; it's about gaining clarity and strength to move forward. That shift—from resisting to adapting—is situational acceptance in action. It's the mindset that turns challenges into opportunities for growth, freeing you from helplessness and opening doors to new possibilities.

Let me take you back to an incident from my own life. It was a sunny morning, and my wife and I were on our way to an event we had been looking forward to for weeks. We had planned everything down to the last detail. But as life would have it, our car broke down in the middle of nowhere. There we were, stranded on the side of the road, with no immediate help in sight. At first, frustration took over. The plans we had so carefully made now seemed like they were slipping through our fingers. But as we sat there, we realized something important: we couldn't control the situation, but we could control how we responded to it.

Instead of dwelling on what we couldn't change, we decided to adapt. We found a mechanic nearby, called for assistance, and while we waited, we made the most of that unexpected pause. We chatted, laughed, and even found a small roadside tea stall where we shared a cup of chai. What could have been a miserable day turned into a reminder of how powerful acceptance can be. It taught us to let go of what was out of our hands and to find small joys even in the middle of a setback.

Situational acceptance starts with a simple but often overlooked truth: you can't control everything. Traffic jams happen. Flights get delayed. Rain can ruin a picnic. When you accept this reality, you free yourself from the weight of frustration and open yourself up to new possibilities. It's not about resigning to fate or being passive. Instead, it's about acknowledging the situation and making a conscious choice to respond positively.

For example, you might be late to a family function because of an unexpected work emergency. Instead of berating yourself for being late, focus on making the most of the time you do have with your loved ones. Situational acceptance doesn't mean you're happy with the disruption, but it allows you to move forward without being bogged down by guilt or regret.

Acceptance also makes room for adaptability. In my professional life, I've experienced corporate mergers, acquisitions, and even separations—three major transitions that, at first, felt overwhelming. During the first one, I worried constantly about job security and the unknown future. But by the time the next transition came around, I had learned to approach the situation with a positive mindset. I reminded myself that change is an inevitable part of business and life. Instead of resisting it, I embraced it, focusing on how I could grow and contribute in the new environment. This shift in perspective made all the difference. I was no longer a passive participant in the change but an active one, ready to adapt and thrive.

Situational acceptance isn't about ignoring your emotions. It's natural to feel upset or disappointed when plans go awry. What matters is what you do after that initial reaction. Acknowledge your feelings, but don't let them control you. Instead, redirect your energy toward what's within your control. Can't fix the situation immediately? Look for ways to minimize its impact. Can't change the outcome? Learn from the experience and carry those lessons forward.

Sometimes, the key to acceptance lies in reframing the situation. For instance, a delayed meeting might feel like an inconvenience at first. But could it also be an opportunity to review your notes and refine your points? A missed train might force you to take a longer route, but it could also introduce you to a charming little cafe you'd never noticed before. When you shift your focus from what's wrong to what's possible, you'll find that even the most frustrating moments can hold hidden blessings.

To practice situational acceptance, start with small tweaks:

- **Acknowledge the reality** of the situation without resistance. Recognize what you can and cannot change.

- **Accept the outcomes** gracefully. If you're late to an event, acknowledge it without dwelling on the "what ifs." Focus on making the most of the time you have.

- **Reframe the challenge.** Look for positives or opportunities within the setback. This shift in perspective can turn obstacles into stepping stones.

As you cultivate this mindset, you'll begin to see how acceptance creates a foundation for inner peace and external adaptability. And in those moments when life feels overwhelming, remember: you may not be able to control the storm, but you can choose how you weather it.

With each challenge, we learn and grow, and acceptance becomes a skill that reshapes our lives.

Thought Leaders on Acceptance

Life is unpredictable, and setbacks are inevitable. But when you approach these moments with acceptance, you'll find that they lose their power to derail you. Instead, they become opportunities to grow, adapt, and discover new paths. Situational acceptance is a practice, one that builds resilience and equips you to handle life's twists and turns with grace.

As we reflect on acceptance, let's revisit the wisdom shared earlier: Eckhart Tolle reminds us that "Acceptance looks like a passive state, but in reality, it brings something entirely new into this world." This peace, rooted in acceptance, isn't passive resignation but a powerful shift that allows us to navigate challenges with clarity and strength.

Similarly, George Orwell's words echo this sentiment: "Happiness can exist only in acceptance." Happiness doesn't stem from avoiding difficulties but from embracing them, adapting, and finding meaning within the experience.

Nathaniel Branden also offers a valuable perspective: "The first step toward change is awareness. The second step is acceptance." Awareness allows us to see things clearly, while acceptance enables us to move forward, grounded in reality. Together, these steps lay the foundation for meaningful change and growth.

However, practicing acceptance doesn't mean surrendering to every situation. It's simply discerning what is worth your energy and what is beyond your control. For instance, while it's essential to adapt to circumstances, it's equally important to recognize when acceptance has veered into unhealthy resignation.

This balance—accepting reality while maintaining a growth-oriented mindset—ensures that acceptance becomes a tool for empowerment rather than complacency.

Acceptance aligns seamlessly with the themes of happiness we've explored throughout this journey. It complements self-accountability by encouraging us to take responsibility for our actions and reactions. It works hand-in-hand with gratitude by helping us focus on what we have rather than what we lack. And it fosters resilience by teaching us to adapt and thrive, even in the face of uncertainty.

As you integrate these lessons into your life, acceptance becomes more than a practice—it becomes a lens through which you approach every challenge and opportunity. It's not the end of the road but the beginning of a journey toward navigating life's complexities with grace, authenticity, and purpose.

So the next time you face a challenge, pause and ask yourself: 'What can I accept here, and how can I respond with purpose?' Acceptance becomes easy when you respond to situations and difficult when you only react. You might be surprised by how much peace and strength acceptance can bring!

Chapter 12

THE DETOXIFICATION

It's past midnight, and the soft glow of your phone is the only light in the room. The house is silent. You're lying in bed, phone in hand, scrolling through an endless stream of updates, videos, and notifications. You tell yourself it'll be the last video, the last scroll, just a few more minutes, but before you know it, another hour has slipped away. The room feels heavier somehow, the silence deeper, and instead of feeling entertained, you're left with a restless mind. Your eyes sting, your body craves sleep, but your thoughts are tangled in the endless stream of updates, memes, and news.

How often has this familiar scenario played out for you? Too often, perhaps.

We've all been there—that quiet pull of the screen that promises entertainment, connection, or even a fleeting sense of accomplishment. Yet, instead of feeling fulfilled, you're left with a nagging emptiness. You set the phone down, frustrated, wondering why it's so hard to stop. This is the power—and the problem—of our digital lives: it gives so much, yet sometimes, it takes away more than it provides.

It's a kind of overload—a buildup of virtual toxins in the mind, much like the physical toxins our body accumulates. And just as we periodically cleanse our bodies to feel lighter and healthier, we need the same for our minds. Throughout this book, we've explored the many factors that chip away at happiness—negative thoughts, procrastination, materialism—and how to rid yourself of them. Digital overload is no different. It quietly fills your time and space until there's no room left for clarity, presence, or real connection.

Mental detoxification is not about abandoning technology but about using it purposefully. It's about clearing out the distractions, comparisons, and superficial connections that keep us from what truly matters. Technology has transformed life in incredible ways, making the world more reachable and accessible.

Technology is neutral; it's how we use it that defines its impact.

When used wisely, technology is a powerful tool for growth, connection, and learning. But when left unchecked, it can trap us in a cycle of distraction, comparison, and detachment from the world around us. Our obsession with mobile phones, screens, and digital content reminds me of a line from "Hotel California" by the Eagles: "We are all just prisoners here of our own device." In today's age of digital overload, that lyric feels more relevant than ever.

Breaking free from this cycle isn't just about managing your time—it's about reclaiming your peace of mind. Imagine a life where you're not stuck in the endless scroll but actively directing your attention toward what truly matters. It starts with recognizing when technology serves you and when it begins to take over. From there, you can take intentional steps to set boundaries, regain control, and restore balance.

The Power to Disconnect

Technology has become an inseparable part of our lives, intertwining itself into nearly every moment of the day. It wakes us up with alarms, keeps us connected to friends and family, and provides endless entertainment and information. But somewhere along the way, this tool meant to serve us started to control us. The habit of checking notifications immediately upon waking, or the reflex to reach for your phone during even the smallest lull, has turned into a cycle that feels almost impossible to break.

Digital exposure, while offering convenience and connectivity, often comes at a hidden cost. Hours spent in front of screens take their toll—on your eyes, your sleep, your posture, and, most importantly, your mind. Anxiety creeps in as you compare your life to curated versions of others' on social media. The constant buzz of updates fractures your attention span, making it harder to focus on meaningful tasks. And at the end of the day, the question remains: does all this connectivity actually make you feel more connected?

It's not about abandoning technology altogether; it's about reclaiming control. The power to disconnect lies in recognizing when digital exposure begins to harm rather than help. Think about how often you've reached for your phone without even realizing it, scrolling through feeds not because you wanted to, but because you felt compelled to. This isn't mindfulness—it's habit. And breaking that habit starts with understanding its impact on your well-being.

When you give yourself permission to disconnect, you create space—space for clarity, focus, and meaningful connections. It's not just about avoiding harm; it's about embracing the benefits of a life where you set the terms for how technology fits in. Instead of being a consumer of endless content, you become the architect of your time and attention.

Social media, for example, has immense potential. It can be a platform for growth, learning, and meaningful interactions. Yet, when used unwisely, it becomes a trap, pulling you into a vortex of comparison, anxiety, and constant consumption.

The difference lies in intention—are you in control, or has the tool taken control of you?

Let's consider the mental and physical toll excessive screen time can take. Anxiety and depression are often linked to social media overuse. Poor sleep, caused by endless scrolling late into the night, leaves you exhausted the next day. Even your physical health is affected—strained eyes, stiff necks, and sedentary habits are all consequences of living life through a screen. Recognizing these effects is the first step toward change.

The power to disconnect isn't about denying yourself the benefits of technology; it's about deciding how and when to engage with it. When you take control, things become manageable. You establish a routine that prioritizes what matters—rest, relationships, and real-world experiences. You stop letting notifications dictate your day and start setting boundaries that protect your well-being.

Imagine waking up and choosing not to check your phone first thing. Instead, you spend a few quiet moments planning your day or simply enjoying the morning light. Imagine an evening spent in meaningful conversation, uninterrupted by the ping of a message. These small changes can transform how you experience life, allowing you to fully engage with the present moment.

When you step back from excessive digital exposure, you reclaim something invaluable: your peace of mind.

It's not always easy to disconnect in a world that values constant availability, but it's worth it. Each time you choose to unplug, you're choosing clarity over chaos, presence over distraction, and happiness over the fleeting satisfaction of a like or a comment. And when you understand the true cost of staying endlessly connected, the question isn't whether to disconnect—it's how to start reclaiming your life.

Digital Overload

The psychological effects of constant connectivity are far-reaching, shaping how we think and how we feel and interact with the world around us. Think of someone lost in their screen, scrolling endlessly, seeking validation through likes and comments. Perhaps this isn't a distant image—it could be someone you know well, or even a reflection of your own habits.

The curated perfection of social media feeds creates a mirage—a life that seems achievable but leaves you doubting your own reality. It's a cycle that many find themselves in, yet few recognize the toll it's taking until they feel completely overwhelmed.

Being connected to the digital world brings undeniable benefits: the ability to stay informed, productive, and socially engaged. But when this connection becomes a constant presence, it shifts from empowering to exhausting. The term "FOMO," or fear of missing out, encapsulates one of the most pervasive psychological costs of digital overload. Scrolling through updates, seeing others achieve milestones, travel, or enjoy moments of joy can trigger unnecessary self-comparison. It plants seeds of inadequacy where none existed before, making you feel like you're always falling short.

This isn't the only consequence. Constant connectivity impacts your ability to focus and leaves your attention fractured. Notifications buzz, timelines refresh, and the endless flood of content demands more and more of your mental energy. Over time, this erodes your ability to be present in the moment, diminishing the quality of your relationships and even your ability to enjoy simple pleasures. And yet, many remain trapped, checking their phones reflexively, as though compelled by an invisible force. It's not just a bad habit; it's a behavioral addiction rooted in the need for instant gratification.

Consider the concept of "selfitis." When front-facing cameras became ubiquitous, taking selfies seemed like harmless fun. But as people began obsessively capturing and sharing images of themselves, a pattern emerged. Researchers coined the term to describe a condition where individuals feel compelled to post selfies constantly, seeking validation from likes and comments. This behavior, categorized into stages—borderline, acute, and chronic—is a stark reminder of how digital platforms can manipulate our need for affirmation, turning a tool into a crutch.

Another term that captures the modern condition is "nomophobia," or the fear of being without one's phone. Think about the last time you left your phone at home or ran out of battery. Did it leave you feeling uneasy, disconnected, or even panicked? This behavioral addiction to mobile devices stems from their design: constant pings, vibrations, and updates that keep pulling you back. It's no accident; the platforms are designed to capture your attention and keep you engaged for as long as possible. But this engagement comes at a cost—a life spent more online than offline.

The effects of this are so pronounced that Oxford even added a new term to its dictionary in 2024: "brain rot." Defined as the mental deterioration caused by consuming trivial or low-quality online content, this term highlights the insidious nature of doom-scrolling, short-form videos, and other addictive digital habits. Hours of engaging with unchallenging material leave you feeling mentally drained, yet unfulfilled. Instead of enriching your life, this content erodes your ability to think critically, focus deeply, or find joy in meaningful activities.

On one of my bike trips (yes, the same one you're familiar with by now), I met a shopkeeper who told me a story I'll never forget. A customer had walked in, obsessed with creating and posting short videos for social media. The shopkeeper noted how the person had purchased equipment to improve their content, but also confided in taking anti-anxiety pills. The irony was striking: the individual's curated, happy online persona hid the strain of maintaining appearances. This shopkeeper, having experienced the addictive nature of social media himself, had opted for a simpler, less connected life. Using a basic feature phone, he found it easier to focus on his work and personal well-being. His story is a reminder that breaking free from the digital matrix is possible, and often necessary, for mental clarity.

The illusion of connectivity is another facet of digital overload.

Virtual interactions can create a sense of belonging, but they rarely match the depth of real-world connections. A heartfelt conversation with a friend or a shared laugh over dinner provides a level of satisfaction that no comment thread or online exchange can replicate. The fleeting high of virtual validation often leaves an emptiness behind, one that only grows with repeated exposure. Understanding this illusion is the first step toward reclaiming genuine connections.

As you begin to recognize the psychological toll of constant connectivity, you're better equipped to address it. Digital overload isn't a permanent state; it's a challenge to overcome.

The key lies in shifting your focus—from the endless noise of online interactions to the meaningful, grounding experiences of the real world. This understanding is the foundation of change. The next step is to take actionable steps toward breaking free from the grip of digital dependence and rediscovering the richness of an unplugged life.

Practicing Digital Detox

A few months ago, I decided to try an experiment. My day began as it usually did, with a phone in my hand. Notifications buzzed every few minutes, pulling my attention in a dozen different directions. Messages, emails, endless updates—it felt like I was juggling responsibilities without ever fully grasping any of them. By the evening, my head was heavy, my focus scattered, and my energy drained. The next day, I made a deliberate choice: no phone, no notifications, no screens unless absolutely necessary. The change was startling. Without the constant interruptions, my mind felt clearer, my day stretched longer, and for the first time in a while, I felt present. That single day taught me the power of a digital detox—a reminder that technology should enhance life, not control it.

Billy Cox once said, "Technology should improve your life, not become your life." This sentiment captures the essence of digital detox. In a world where screens dominate our waking hours, reclaiming that balance begins with small, intentional steps. One of the simplest ways to start is by time-boxing your digital world. Set aside specific times in the day for checking emails or scrolling social media, and stick to those boundaries. Turning off non-essential notifications can also be a game-changer. The constant buzz of updates creates an illusion of urgency, but most of these alerts can wait. Scheduling device-free hours—perhaps during meals or before bedtime—allows you to reconnect with yourself and those around you. It's about regaining control over your time, ensuring that technology serves you, not the other way around.

Another practical approach is finding meaningful alternatives to screen time. Think of the last time you felt truly refreshed. Chances are, it wasn't after hours of scrolling but after engaging in something tangible—reading a book, walking in nature, or enjoying a hobby. The Japanese practice of "Shinrin-yoku," or forest bathing, emphasizes the therapeutic benefits of immersing oneself in nature. Even a short walk among trees can reduce stress and improve mental clarity. Jane Goodall's words ring true here: "Take time to disconnect and find the wonder in the world around you. Nature does not require a Wi-Fi connection." Whether it's gardening, painting, or simply sitting outside with a cup of tea, these moments of unplugged mindfulness can rejuvenate your spirit in ways no screen ever could.

Self-control and awareness are the backbone of any digital detox. The key is identifying the triggers that pull you into excessive screen time. Is it boredom? Stress? The need for distraction? Once you're aware of these patterns, you can consciously choose healthier responses. For instance, if you find yourself doom-scrolling out of habit, replace that time with a simple ritual, like journaling or stretching. When stress tempts you to reach for your phone, try deep breathing or meditation instead. These small shifts in behavior can break the cycle of digital dependence and create space for meaningful experiences.

The beauty of a digital detox lies in its simplicity.

It's not a big drastic change but simple, consistent, intentional choices. Each step—whether it's silencing notifications, spending time in nature, or practicing mindfulness—brings you closer to a life where you're in control. And as you begin to embrace these practices, you'll realize that the rewards extend far beyond clearer minds and calmer days. They lead to a richer, more fulfilling connection with the world around you, reminding you that the best moments are the ones lived fully, not filtered through a screen.

Real Happiness Beyond Screens

Step away from the screen for a moment and think back to your own childhood.

Remember those carefree evenings spent playing cricket in the neighborhood park? The sound of a well-hit ball cutting through the air, the laughter of friends echoing as they chased it down, and the parents who cheered, their phones tucked away and forgotten. It wasn't extraordinary—it was joy in its purest form.

These moments remind us of what it feels like to truly connect with the world around us, unburdened by the pull of screens. Think back to simpler times, when evenings were spent outside playing, shouting for runs, and sharing laughs with friends. There were no notifications to check, no reels to scroll—just pure, unfiltered joy.

What changed then?

Homework turned into online assignments, social media became a second home, and before you knew it, screens weren't just a part of life—they became the center of it. Work followed suit. Meetings moved to virtual platforms, jobs demanded constant digital engagement, and even leisure time often felt like an extension of screen time. The boundaries blurred, and the digital world seeped into every corner of life.

But something remarkable happens when you make the shift and engage with the real world.

Conversations carry more weight when they're held face-to-face. A shared meal with loved ones tastes richer when it's not interrupted by scrolling. These moments aren't fleeting; they leave a lasting imprint, deepening bonds and building empathy. Unlike the virtual world's transient likes and comments, real-world connections create memories that stay with you.

Think about it—10 likes on your post might feel disappointing, but if 10 people in real life told you they liked your outfit, it would make your day!

Engaging in real-world activities isn't just good for the soul; it's transformative for the mind and body. Imagine stepping outside for a walk after hours spent indoors. The crisp air fills your lungs, the sound of leaves crunching underfoot centers your thoughts, and for a moment, life feels wonderfully simple.

Activities like these don't demand perfection or performance; they invite you to be present. This presence enhances mental clarity, reduces stress, and fosters mindfulness—all crucial ingredients for happiness.

Real-world engagement also strengthens practical life skills. Consider how team-building in an actual game of cricket differs from playing a virtual one. On the field, teamwork isn't about quick reactions or avatars; it's about communication, trust, and shared effort. These are skills that carry over into every area of life—work, relationships, and personal growth. Beyond teamwork, real-world engagement fosters better time management and prioritization. In the real world, deadlines are tangible, consequences immediate. These factors naturally counter procrastination and encourage you to act with clarity and purpose.

I remember a lesson I learned on the same bike trip I've shared throughout this book. A fellow rider, who had faced significant financial losses due to procrastinating necessary home repairs, shared a practice that transformed his outlook. He described treating his helmet as a personal studio—a space to think clearly, sing freely, and have positive self-talks without interruption. It wasn't just avoiding distractions; it was creating intentional moments to reconnect with himself. His story was a powerful reminder that even small, deliberate steps toward disconnecting can create space for reflection and joy.

The world is an incredible teacher.

When you step away from screens and engage with life directly, you're opening yourself up to lessons no algorithm can replicate. You learn resilience from missed trains, empathy from heartfelt conversations, and joy from spontaneous adventures. These experiences, unfiltered and genuine, shape a happiness that's lasting and real. It's the kind of happiness that comes from being fully present—in your relationships, your surroundings, and your own skin.

Reconnecting with the real world isn't about rejecting technology; it's about reclaiming balance. Set aside time to join a community activity, whether it's volunteering, attending a local event, or participating in a neighborhood game. Make a conscious effort to prioritize face-to-face interactions over virtual ones. Whether it's meeting a friend for chai or sitting down for dinner with family, these moments foster deeper connections and create memories worth cherishing.

As you lean into these practices, you'll find that the rewards go beyond personal satisfaction. Real happiness is contagious. When you're fully present and engaged, you inspire those around you to do the same. It's a ripple effect that transforms not just your life but the lives of those you touch.

Life offline offers a richness that no screen can replicate. It's found in the warmth of shared laughter, the thrill of spontaneous adventures, and the peace of a quiet moment spent in nature. These experiences remind us that the real world, with all its imperfections and unpredictability, is where true happiness resides.

Step away from the screen, look up, and rediscover the world waiting for you—a world brimming with connection, purpose, and joy.

Chapter 13

PROCESS VS. OUTCOME

Who doesn't love a good cup of chai?

You're standing in your kitchen, the familiar smell wafting through the air as the tea leaves swirl in the boiling water. You add milk and sugar, perhaps a touch of ginger or cardamom, and let it simmer until the flavors meld together. Every step feels intentional, yet every cup is slightly different. Some days it's perfectly balanced, with just the right amount of sweetness. Other times, you might get distracted for a moment, and the milk boils over, leaving the tea with a bitterness you hadn't planned for.

It's such a small ritual, but it reveals something important. The process matters—each step influences the result. And while the outcome is satisfying, much of the joy lies in making it.

Life works the same way.

We're often so focused on the final product—the finished project, the promotion, the personal milestone—that we forget to appreciate the effort it took to get there. The joy isn't confined to the moment you sip the perfect cup of chai; it's in the journey of making it, experimenting, and learning what works best.

Take a moment to reflect on your own life. Think about a milestone you're proud of—acing an exam, completing a challenging project at work, or running your first 5K. The feeling of accomplishment when you crossed the finish line was rewarding, but how long did it last? A week? Maybe two? And then your mind likely shifted to the next goal. Now think about the time leading up to that moment. The late nights spent studying, the hours of brainstorming and revisions, the early mornings and practice runs. Those moments, though often overlooked, were filled with small victories, lessons, and growth.

The truth is, the in-between moments carry far more meaning than we often give them credit for. They're the quiet spaces where resilience is built, creativity flourishes, and joy resides. They're the thread that weaves together the larger story of who you're becoming. Happiness works in much the same way. It's not a trophy waiting at the finish line; it's scattered along the path, ready to be noticed in each step, each effort, each lesson learned.

This isn't to say results don't matter—they do. But when your happiness hinges solely on outcomes, it becomes fragile.

A missed goal, a less-than-perfect result, can leave you feeling deflated. Focusing on the journey, however, gives you something more enduring. It allows you to find satisfaction and meaning in every step you take, even the missteps. It's about recognizing that the struggles, the progress, and the growth are what truly shape your experience.

So, what does it truly mean to embrace the journey rather than just focus on the destination? It begins with learning to appreciate and fall in love with the process itself.

Loving the Process

Falling in love with the process means embracing every step of the path, recognizing that each moment contributes to your growth and joy. Happiness doesn't wait at the end of the road—it's found in how you walk it, one step at a time.

When you think about the joy in making chai, it isn't just the final sip that brings satisfaction. It's the small decisions along the way—choosing the right amount of sugar, waiting for the milk to foam just enough, or experimenting with a hint of cinnamon. The act of making it, with all its little tweaks and adjustments, carries its own joy. This same principle holds true for every meaningful pursuit in life.

Focusing on the process rather than fixating on the result is a mindset shift that can transform how you experience growth, success, and happiness. Consider this: when you achieve something significant, whether it's a promotion, completing a challenging project, or crossing the finish line of a race, how long does the high of accomplishment last? A week? Maybe two? And yet, the months or years spent preparing for that moment—the late nights, the trial and error, the quiet victories along the way—hold more lasting value than we often realize. Those moments of effort and learning are where growth truly happens. They're where life happens.

Take, for example, an athlete training for a race. The finish line might last seconds, but the process leading up to it is filled with hundreds of hours of practice, sacrifice, and incremental progress. The same is true for musicians or artists who rehearse tirelessly for a performance that might last just a couple of hours. Their joy doesn't come solely from the applause but from the discipline, the habits, and the creativity nurtured during their preparation. These stories remind us that happiness and fulfillment are not found only in the final applause—they're embedded in the rhythm of the practice itself.

The beauty of focusing on the process is that it allows you to redefine success.

Success is no longer a single destination to reach but a collection of meaningful moments and experiences along the way. When you love the process, every step—even the challenging ones—feels purposeful. You're not waiting for happiness to appear at the finish line; you're finding it in the effort, in the learning, and in the perseverance.

Think about your own journey. Perhaps you've started journaling, inspired by an earlier chapter in this book. The goal might be to become more self-aware, but the act of writing each day—capturing your thoughts, reflecting on your emotions, and noticing patterns—is where the transformation lies. Journaling itself is the process, and it's through that process that self-awareness begins to take root. Without embracing the practice, the outcome wouldn't be possible.

Every act, big or small, follows a process. Buying a car, pursuing a degree, or even deciding what to cook for dinner involves steps and decisions that shape the outcome. When you pay attention to these steps and allow yourself to be fully present in them, the experience becomes richer. You start noticing the details that would otherwise go overlooked, and those details often bring moments of unexpected joy. For example, when buying a car, it's not just the satisfaction of driving it home; it's the research, the test drives, the conversations, and the anticipation that make it a fulfilling journey.

Loving the process leads to long-lasting joy. It builds resilience because you're no longer dependent on outcomes to feel good about your efforts. It helps you develop a growth mindset, as discussed earlier in the chapter on acceptance, by encouraging you to see every step as an opportunity to learn and improve. It builds a 360-degree understanding of what it takes to achieve something meaningful, allowing you to appreciate both the effort and the result.

Most importantly, embracing the process allows you to find happiness in the smallest of steps. Whether it's perfecting a recipe, mastering a new skill, or simply learning to pause and enjoy the moment, the joy lies in the doing. It's about celebrating progress rather than waiting for perfection. And when you begin to love the process, you create a foundation of happiness that's steady, enduring, and rooted in the present moment.

So, what does it mean to truly fall in love with the process? It means waking up every day with the intention to grow, knowing that each effort contributes to something greater. It means letting go of the pressure to reach the destination and instead focusing on the beauty of the steps that lead you there. Happiness isn't something you achieve when you cross the finish line; it's what you build, step by step, as you move forward.

Embracing Setbacks

You've probably heard the saying, "What doesn't kill you makes you stronger." But how often do we actually live by that? Setbacks can feel like failures at first, but when we allow ourselves to reflect, we can see that they often set us on the path to something far greater.

Embracing setbacks means more than enduring hardship; it means recognizing the valuable lessons they often bring. Imagine a world without setbacks. What would that mean for us? Without challenges, there would be no growth, no opportunity for resilience, and no real progress. Life would become stagnant, and we would miss out on the deep lessons setbacks provide.

As Swami Vivekananda wisely said, "In a day, when you don't come across any problems, you can be sure that you are travelling on the wrong path." This perspective is liberating. It suggests that setbacks aren't signs of failure, but markers on the right path. They tell us that we're engaged, that we're pushing boundaries, and that we're learning. Setbacks, in this light, are just another word for opportunities. They are a signal that we're in the process of growing, and that growth is what ultimately brings happiness.

I remember one of my most significant setbacks during my academic years. I had put in hours of studying, hoping to excel in an important exam, but when the results came out, I saw that I had scored well below my expectations. The disappointment was crushing. The weight of those grades felt unbearable, and for a while, it seemed like my whole world had crumbled. It was as though the success I had imagined for myself was slipping through my fingers. But as the initial sadness passed, my perspective began to shift. My elder brother, whom I admire deeply, came to my side with a box of sweets to lighten the mood. He told me, "The world hasn't ended. These marks are just numbers. They can't control your fate. Learn from this, and grow." In that moment, his words planted a seed of resilience in me. What I had seen as a failure, he saw as an opportunity for growth. That setback, which felt like the end, turned out to be the beginning of an entirely new path, one filled with opportunities I had never considered before.

Had I not faced that disappointment, I wouldn't have been open to exploring those new possibilities. I might not have learned how to handle failure, adapt, and find new ways to move forward. That moment, as painful as it was, became the turning point that reshaped my understanding of success. It wasn't the result that mattered—it was the process of learning, reflecting, and using the setback as a stepping stone.

This idea of embracing setbacks is beautifully illustrated in the story of Sachin Tendulkar, one of the greatest cricketers of all time. In 2004, during a series against Australia, Sachin was dismissed three times playing his signature cover drive—a shot that had defined his career. It was a major setback, not just for him, but for the entire team. But instead of being discouraged, Sachin used that failure to adapt and evolve. In the following match, he scored a magnificent 241 not out, but what made this innings extraordinary wasn't just the runs—it was the way he played without a single cover drive. He took the lesson from his setbacks and changed his approach. He demonstrated the power of resilience, discipline, and adaptability. This innings became one of the most iconic performances of his career, proving that setbacks aren't failures—they are opportunities to refine our approach and push ourselves further.

What Sachin teaches us is that setbacks can be transformative.

They can be the catalysts that push us to become better versions of ourselves. When we face challenges, we often find new strengths within us, ones we never knew existed. Every setback presents us with a chance to build a deeper understanding of ourselves and our goals. The key is to embrace those moments, not as hindrances, but as integral parts of our journey.

Life is full of hustle and struggle, and there will always be setbacks—whether they're personal, professional, or emotional. But the real work, the work that leads to lasting happiness, comes in how we respond to those setbacks.

Do we let them defeat us, or do we use them to propel us forward? If we can learn to embrace these challenges, we begin to see them not as obstacles, but as essential pieces of our growth story. It's through these struggles that we build resilience, and it's through resilience that we build happiness. Life is a constant series of learning, adapting, and overcoming, and each setback is just a part of that process.

So, the next time you face a setback, don't see it as a failure. See it as a chance to refine your approach, grow stronger, and adapt. It's through these moments that we discover the true meaning of resilience—and it's through resilience that we build lasting happiness.

Saying No

When we talk about resilience, we usually mean how well we handle life's challenges. But just as important as bouncing back is the way we shape our surroundings—the space we grow in and the energy we let into our lives.

Take a moment and think about it: you could be fighting your own battles, learning from failures, and pushing yourself forward, but if everything around you feels overwhelming—if you're saying yes to every request and obligation—how much space is left for your growth? How much energy do you really have to embrace the lessons from those setbacks?

If every day feels like a sprint—if you're constantly checking off to-do lists, responding to messages, managing work, family, and social commitments—when do you actually get to focus on yourself? When do you have time to learn, to grow, to really pause and think about where you want to go next?

When your mind is cluttered with distractions, it becomes harder to find clarity. The constant noise of life makes it difficult to connect with what truly matters to you.

Now, here's where we often miss the mark: We think that saying yes is what makes us busy, productive, or even valuable to others. But the truth is, the power lies in knowing when to say no. And saying no isn't just about rejecting things—it's about consciously creating space for what truly matters.

It's as simple as this: You're sitting down to a meal at the end of a long day, and your plate is already overflowing. The food is there, but you can barely taste the flavors because it's too much—too heavy, too many choices, too many distractions. That's what life can feel like when we say yes to everything. We're constantly filling our plate, never really savoring anything. And what we need is to step back, look at our plate, and say, "This, this is what I really need. The rest can wait."

Remember the process of making tea we talked about? Imagine carefully brewing a cup of chai—the water boiling gently, the tea leaves steeping just right, the aroma of spices filling the air. But then, you add too much sugar, and suddenly it's cloyingly sweet. Or you toss in extra ginger, and now it's overpoweringly sharp. That perfect balance is gone, and what could have been a comforting cup is ruined.

Life works the same way. If you keep saying "yes" to everything—every request, every opportunity, every demand—you risk throwing off your balance. Too much of anything, no matter how good it seems, can overwhelm you. Learning to say "no" is like measuring each ingredient with care. It's about respecting your limits and creating space for what truly matters, so your life remains rich and fulfilling, not chaotic and overburdened.

Paulo Coelho, in his wisdom, once said, "When you say YES to others, make sure you are not saying NO to yourself." That line isn't just a good quote to hang on the wall—it's a reminder to us all. How many times have you said yes to a friend, a colleague, or even a family member, only to realize later that you've stretched yourself so thin, you don't have the energy for the things that truly make you happy? How many times have you put others' needs before your own, and in doing so, neglected your own well-being?

It's a difficult thing to do, isn't it?

To put yourself first, to say no without guilt. We all know the fear of missing out, the feeling that saying no might disappoint someone, or worse, make us feel unimportant. But when you constantly give in to everyone else's demands, you lose sight of your own needs. You forget to ask yourself: What do I need right now to feel good? To feel balanced? To feel fulfilled?

Warren Buffet, one of the wealthiest men in the world, also understands this principle well. He once said, "The difference between successful people and really successful people is that really successful people say no to almost everything." At first, that might sound counterintuitive. Shouldn't success be about taking every opportunity that comes your way? But Buffet's point is simple yet profound: Saying no isn't about being unkind or shutting people out—it's about being deliberate, being intentional. It's about knowing that time is limited, and the energy we give out is finite. So, instead of trying to do everything, we need to focus on what truly matters.

When you start saying no, you aren't rejecting life—you're choosing the right things to say yes to. You're clearing away the clutter and creating space for your real priorities. Think of the times you've said no and felt a sense of relief. Maybe it was turning down an unnecessary meeting or skipping a social event you didn't enjoy. After saying no, you had time to do something that nourished your soul—reading, walking, or simply sitting in silence. That's the power of saying no: it gives you the freedom to say yes to what truly makes you happy.

Throughout this book, we've explored how saying no can lead to a life of less stress, less noise, and more focus on what truly matters. We've seen how saying no to distractions, to negative influences, to materialism, and even to perfectionism, can clear the path for happiness. Each no you say is a conscious choice to focus on the things that will bring you long-lasting joy. And in saying no to what doesn't serve you, you open up space for the things that will help you grow, the things that will make you feel alive.

It's time to get comfortable with saying no. Whether it's at work, in your relationships, or in the small day-to-day decisions you make, saying no is a powerful tool for protecting your time, your energy, and your happiness. It's about reclaiming control over your life and making intentional choices that align with who you want to be. And the more you practice this, the easier it becomes. Saying no isn't just a skill—it's a practice that leads to a life where happiness doesn't just show up at the finish line. It's found in the choices you make every single day.

So, the next time you feel the weight of a request, take a moment. Ask yourself, "Does this align with my priorities? Does this serve my happiness?" And if the answer is no, don't be afraid to say it.

Your happiness is worth protecting.

Journey over your Destination

When we start focusing on what really matters, we begin to see that it's not the finish line that makes the journey worthwhile; it's everything that leads up to it. Like I said, it's easy to get caught up in the idea of reaching a destination, but happiness doesn't wait for us at the end of the road. It's the moments along the way that shape us—the people we meet, the connections we forge, the lessons we learn. These are the things that make the journey valuable. It's about learning to appreciate the ride, not just the result.

Think back to something you've experienced where the outcome wasn't clear, but the process was fulfilling nonetheless. For me, I had a chance to experience this first-hand when I participated in a Guinness World Record attempt on January 24th, 2020, just before the pandemic took hold. Over the course of just three or four days, we practiced as a group of 1,046 artists, all of us coming together for the shared purpose of setting a world record. The practice sessions weren't easy—there were hours of coordination, adjusting to different people, synchronizing our efforts—but we all embraced the journey wholeheartedly. We didn't know if we would break the record. The goal was uncertain, but the process of working together, learning from each other, and finding rhythm with people who shared different skill sets was where the true joy lay.

When it was announced that we had achieved the Guinness World Record, it wasn't just about the title. It was the people I met during those few days—musicians, artists, performers—from different walks of life, sharing a moment of growth and collaboration. Even though the record was the end goal, it was the process of coming together, of enjoying each step of the way, that made the experience truly unforgettable. And even now, years later, I still stay in touch with a few of the musicians I met. We share the same passion for music, and that connection is one of the lasting gifts of the experience. If the record had never been broken, it wouldn't have diminished the friendships or the lessons I gained. The experience itself, the journey, became the reward.

This idea of embracing the process instead of fixating solely on the result is something that can be seen in many aspects of life, including relationships. Take marriage, for example. We often think of marriage as a destination—the wedding day. But in reality, marriage is a journey that starts from that very day. In an arranged marriage, the wedding day marks the beginning of the journey, not the end. It's not only two people standing in front of a crowd, promising forever—it's about discovering one another in the days that follow. There's no immediate 'perfect' bond, no instant understanding. The magic comes from learning to compromise, communicate, and grow together. It's in the small moments—the late-night talks, the shared silence, the times when you disagree but still choose to move forward—that the relationship deepens. Marriage isn't a destination, it's an ongoing journey of discovering, understanding, and loving each other, layer by layer. It's in the daily choices you make to build trust, respect, and love that the real beauty of the relationship shines.

The journey is the heart of it all, and without it, the destination wouldn't have the same depth or meaning.

Life, in many ways, mirrors this process.

We all know the ultimate destination—no one can escape the certainty of the end. But what makes life rich isn't that final destination—it's the way we live on our way to it. It's how we learn to embrace the twists and turns, the unexpected detours, and the people we meet along the way. Happiness is not something we wait to achieve at the end; it's something we create and nurture throughout the journey. It is like a companion—always by your side, ready to accompany you through every step, if you choose to see it.

Imagine you've planned a perfect trip. The route is mapped out, everything seems on track, and you're excited. Then, suddenly, heavy rain causes flooding, and the road you were meant to take is closed. Frustration kicks in—this wasn't part of the plan. But what if, instead of dwelling on the setback, you decided to enjoy the ride back? You can't control the floods, but you can control how you respond. That's what acceptance is about. In that moment, the journey becomes more important than the destination. The delays, surprises, and lessons along the way are what make the trip truly memorable. It's often in these unexpected detours that life's best experiences are found.

The journey is found in the quiet, unassuming moments—the unexpected lessons, the connections that shift your perspective, the detours that shape who you are. Life rarely unfolds as planned, and it's in those uncharted turns where meaning often emerges. We spend so much time chasing the destination that we forget to notice the texture of the path beneath our feet and the beauty of what surrounds us.

When plans unravel, pause.

Observe.

Let go of the need for control and allow yourself to embrace the uncertainty. There's depth in the unexpected, wisdom in the interruptions, and joy in simply moving forward. Happiness isn't something to chase; it's found in paying attention to the life unfolding right now, in all its imperfect, unpredictable wonder.

When you focus on the process instead of just the outcome, the journey instead of the destination, you might realize that what you were looking for was there all along—in the journey itself.

Chapter 14

CONTROL AND COMMAND

Life has a funny way of throwing us into situations where things feel completely out of our hands. One minute, everything is falling into place, and the next, we're facing something we didn't see coming. It's in these moments, when we're left wondering how to proceed, that our true power lies. The power to act. The power to choose. The power to control what we can, even when the world around us seems chaotic.

It's easy to feel like a passenger in our own lives, drifting along, hoping for the best. But true strength, and ultimately happiness, comes from realizing one simple truth: we always have the ability to control something. And when we understand what's within our control, that's when we start to harness our own potential, redirecting our energy toward the things that matter most.

Take a moment to think about a time when everything seemed uncertain, when things didn't go as planned. Remember that feeling—the frustration, the anxiety, the uncertainty. Maybe it was a major life event, or perhaps something smaller, like an important meeting or exam that didn't go the way you'd hoped. You felt stuck, didn't you? Out of control. But in those very moments, you still had something under your control. Your response.

You've already seen how setbacks can be turning points—how the right response to failure can change the course of not just a game but an entire career. We spoke earlier about Sachin Tendulkar's 2004 series against

Australia, where his signature cover drive became his downfall. After being dismissed multiple times playing that very shot, he had two choices—keep playing the same way and risk repeating the mistake, or adjust his approach entirely. He chose the latter.

That moment became a defining chapter in his career. The match was a test of character, with expectations soaring as he took the crease. The pressure was immense, but instead of letting past failures dictate his performance, he made a deliberate shift—he would not attempt the cover drive at all. Instead, he focused on the shots he could control. What followed was nothing short of legendary: a stunning 241 not out, a masterclass in resilience and adaptability. The world applauded, not just for the runs he scored, but for the discipline, clarity, and composure he displayed in the face of adversity.

Now, imagine being in his shoes. The weight of previous failures, the scrutiny of millions, the temptation to stick with old habits. It would have been easy to spiral, to let frustration take over. But what Sachin did was simple yet powerful—he controlled his response, not the outcome. The game wasn't lost in the failed shots; it was won in his ability to reassess, refocus, and make the best decision with what was within his reach.

Now, pause for a moment.

Can you recall a time when you had a setback, perhaps a moment when things didn't go according to plan? It could have been something big, or something small—like a missed deadline or an unproductive day. Maybe it was a project that went off track, a meeting that didn't go as expected, or even something personal that challenged you in ways you didn't anticipate. How did you respond? How did you handle it? Did you waste your energy fighting against things you couldn't control, or did you pause and ask yourself what was within your power to change? Just like Sachin, it's about knowing where your energy is best spent. It's about focusing on what you can control, rather than letting what's outside your reach dictate your peace of mind.

You've seen it time and again throughout this book—life doesn't always go as planned. We've all been there: stuck in traffic, watch the most precisely planned plans fall apart unexpectedly, or missed a metaphorical (or literal) bus or two. We've felt stuck with the weight of uncontrollable circumstances, or found ourselves in moments of chaos where the only thing we can control is our response. But what if you could harness that control, just like Sachin did?

What if you could focus on the things you *can* influence, rather than getting stuck in what you can't?

What can you control in your life right now? Think about it. Is it your attitude, your actions, your approach to challenges? When you start to recognize the areas where you have influence and control, that's where true empowerment begins. You stop feeling like a victim of circumstances and start being the architect of your own response.

As you reflect on these moments, think about the concepts we're about to explore—what is truly in your control? How can you focus on the actions you can take, the decisions that are within your grasp, and the mindset you can command? What would happen if you took a moment to understand where your energy is best spent? This is where happiness starts—not in trying to control everything, but in knowing what you can influence, and more importantly, what you can let go of.

Circles of Control

What does your typical daily routine look like? From the moment you wake up to the time you go to bed, you're constantly faced with choices— big and small. Some of these decisions are yours to make, while others are beyond your control. So how do you handle all these moments without feeling overwhelmed? It all comes down to knowing where your energy is best spent.

Everything you deal with falls into one of three circles: control, influence, or concern. Covey's The 7 Habits of Highly Effective People brilliantly describes this framework.

Let's start with control. This is the simplest and most empowering circle: the things that you can directly manipulate. Your thoughts. Your actions. Your reactions. Imagine you're preparing for an important presentation. You can't control how others will react or what questions they'll ask, but you can control how much effort you put into your preparation, the clarity of your message, and the focus of your delivery. This is where self-discipline comes in—acknowledging that your attitude and your behavior are within your command.

Control isn't about suppressing emotions or forcing things into place. It's about accepting that, while you can't control everything around you, your response is yours to manage.

Back in that unforgettable 2004 match against Australia, Sachin Tendulkar faced a tough moment. Three times, he tried to play his signature cover drive, and three times, the ball had him. The easy route would've been to let frustration get the best of him, to let the uncontrollable aspects of the match—the bowler, the pitch conditions, even the expectations of millions of fans—steer him off course. But instead, Tendulkar took control of his response. He chose to step back, reevaluate, and adjust his approach. It wasn't about the shot he couldn't control; it was about how he reacted, how he recalibrated his game. And what happened next? He scored a brilliant 241 not out, a victory of resilience and adaptability. His mastery of his own response, in that moment, was a powerful reminder of the importance of controlling the things you can, and letting go of the things you can't.

Swami Vivekananda, whom I've always admired, teaches us about the profound power of mind control. He emphasized how the ability to control one's thoughts shapes one's destiny. In his words, "Control the mind, and you control your life." The mind, once disciplined, becomes the driving force behind self-awareness and personal growth. Every day is a new opportunity to practice controlling your thoughts—to pause before reacting, to choose peace in moments of conflict, and to reclaim your power from situations that feel uncontrollable.

The more you understand what you can control, the more you empower yourself to create the life you desire.

This brings us to the second circle: influence.

This second circle isn't about direct control, but rather the ability to affect those around you. Influence starts with yourself. It's about how you present yourself to the world—how you model behavior, how you communicate, and how you choose to interact with others. Influence doesn't come from trying to force your way, but from leading by example. It's about showing up with clarity, calm, and consistency. When you're in control of your actions, you automatically influence others, even if it's in subtle ways.

Consider someone widely admired for their leadership—take M.S. Dhoni, for example. While he may not control every detail of a team's success, his influence shapes how the team feels, performs, and grows together. He does this by being present, by maintaining focus, and by inspiring those around him.

Influence works through energy and example.

When you are in control of your thoughts and actions, others begin to notice, and they often follow suit. This is where true leadership emerges—not from trying to control others, but from demonstrating the values you wish to see in the world. You don't have to be the loudest person in the room; sometimes, the most powerful influence comes from the quiet consistency of your own behavior.

Now, let's shift to the third circle: concern.

Concern is the category where we tend to waste the most energy. We all care about things beyond our control: the weather, someone else's behavior, the state of the world. It's natural to feel concerned about these things, but the more we focus on them, the less power we have. Concern often gives rise to stress, anxiety, and frustration because we often try to control things that are beyond our power. Imagine if Sachin had focused on fears of failure, overwhelming expectations, or uncontrollable circumstances—would he have been able to achieve those legendary innings?

Take an example from your own life. Picture yourself stuck in traffic. You see the jam ahead, hear the relentless honking around you, and feel your frustration steadily building. But no matter how much you wish it would clear up, you can't change the traffic. What you can control is your response. You can choose to let go of the frustration, to breathe, to use the time to reflect or listen to music. The traffic is a perfect example of something that falls in the concern circle. It's something we can't change, but we can control how we react to it.

Understanding these circles can drastically reduce unnecessary stress. Recognizing the things outside your control frees you from the burden of trying to change them. For example, you might be concerned about the weather affecting your weekend plans. But you can't control the weather. What you can control is how you plan for the day, how you adjust your expectations, and what attitude you bring to the situation. When you focus on what you can influence and control, the concern circle gets smaller, and you regain your peace of mind.

The more you focus on your circle of control, the less stress and worry you carry. Real transformation happens when you learn to direct your mind—stay disciplined in your thoughts, silence distractions, and train yourself to respond rather than react. That's where Mind Control comes in.

Understanding the three circles—control, influence, and concern—helps us see where to focus our energy. It's easy to get caught up in trying to change things beyond our reach, but real peace comes when we let go of those things and focus on what we can control and influence. This practice not only makes us more effective but also helps build a life rooted in clarity, purpose, and peace.

Once we know where to direct our energy, the next step is harnessing the power of our mind.

Mind Control

What comes to mind when you think of discipline? It's something many of us heard growing up—get up early, follow routines, stay committed. In many Indian households, discipline is a key part of daily life, ingrained in how we approach everything from study to work. But beyond just following schedules, discipline is a tool that empowers us to control what we can: our actions, our focus, and ultimately, our peace of mind. You've probably heard the famous Warren Buffet quote "We do not have to be smarter than the rest; we have to be more disciplined than the rest." Success, in this sense, is not about outsmarting others but mastering the one thing you can always control: your mind.

Think about a time when you faced a tough challenge. Maybe it was a work task that felt impossible or a personal struggle you weren't sure you could get through. What helped you push forward, even when it felt like the odds were against you? Chances are, it wasn't just your skills or resources—it was your mindset. The ability to stay focused, ignore distractions, and keep going even when you felt like giving up. That's where real resilience comes from.

In the example of Sachin's 2004 match, we saw how mastery of the mind is just as important as mastery of technique. After failing three times with his cover drive, he could have let frustration take over. Instead, he stayed focused, adjusted his approach, and chose to control his response. In that moment, it wasn't the match itself that he could control—it was his mind, his thoughts, and his next actions. That's what turned the game around. This kind of discipline is what sets those who succeed apart from those who falter.

Self-discipline isn't limited to rigid control; it involves knowing where to direct your focus. The more disciplined you are in managing your thoughts and actions, the more you gain mastery over your life. Mindfulness plays a significant role in this. It means being aware of your thoughts without being consumed by them. You observe your reactions and choose the one that aligns with your values, purpose, and peace of mind.

Self-discipline and mindfulness are the bedrock of resilience. It's how you weather the storms that life throws at you. Just as Sachin took control of his mind in the heat of the match, you can take control of your mind in any challenging situation. It's not about avoiding discomfort or stress—it's about learning to ride the waves of adversity with focus and grace.

To deepen this practice, start by reflecting on how your mind works. It's easy to let your thoughts run wild, especially when emotions are running high. But when you become mindful of your thoughts, you can separate yourself from them. You stop identifying with every passing feeling or judgment. Instead, you start to see them as fleeting experiences that don't define you. This awareness allows you to make intentional choices, no longer driven by impulsive reactions but by clarity and purpose.

Take this book, for example. The very act of writing this was an exercise in mind control and discipline. At times, it felt like the words wouldn't come, or the direction wasn't clear. But through hours of focus, of quieting the distractions in my mind, and of committing to the process, the words eventually found their place. Writing isn't about inspiration alone—it's about the discipline to sit down, to stay present, and to push through the mental barriers. The same is true for every challenge you face.

When we allow ourselves to be controlled by our fleeting emotions or external chaos, we surrender our power. But when we take control of our mind—when we pause, breathe, and realign with our values—we reclaim our ability to respond in a way that serves our highest good. This is where happiness resides: in the clarity, focus, and calm that come with a disciplined mind.

Through mindfulness, you create space between stimulus and reaction. Instead of jumping to conclusions or acting on impulse, you step back. You breathe. You listen. You choose. And in that space, lies the power to control your destiny. The more you practice, the more resilient you become—able to weather any storm with a sense of peace and purpose.

In every moment of uncertainty, the key to moving forward isn't found in controlling the world around you, but in controlling how you react to it.

Self-discipline and mindfulness give you the tools to do this. They allow you to face adversity not with fear or frustration, but with calm and clarity. It's a practice, not an overnight transformation. But as you continue to hone this skill, you'll find that life becomes less about managing the chaos and more about finding peace within it.

Embracing Chaos

Do you remember the year when everything changed overnight?

One evening, markets were crowded, the scent of fresh samosas and chai filling the air, and conversations flowed freely at roadside stalls. The next morning, silence took over. Train stations that once carried millions stood deserted, shops pulled down their shutters indefinitely, and families found themselves confined to their homes, uncertain of what lay ahead.

The sudden shift was unsettling—the routine of daily life disrupted in ways that had never been seen before. At first, the quiet was unnerving, the unknown overwhelming. But as time passed, people found ways to adapt. Homes became offices, kitchens turned into makeshift classrooms, and communities found new ways to connect—from sharing resources to checking in on each other's well-being. The chaos was still there, but people learned to move through it, adjusting their expectations and responses rather than fighting against what was beyond their control.

This is what it means to embrace chaos—not to eliminate it, but to move through it without losing yourself. The pandemic was a massive example, but we experience smaller versions of this every day. The missed deadline, the sudden change in plans, the unexpected traffic jam that throws off your schedule. In these moments, you have two choices: fight against the uncontrollable and exhaust yourself in frustration, or shift your focus to what you can manage—your response, your attitude, and your next step.

When you have a controlled mind, when you learn to remain calm and practice responding instead of reacting, even the most unpredictable situations lose their power over you. The discipline we've discussed earlier is what helps you navigate these moments.

Without it, chaos can consume you.

With it, you remain grounded despite the storm.

How often do you let the uncontrollable dictate your emotions? How much stress do you carry because you are resisting something that is already happening? The truth is, resisting chaos only adds to its weight. Acceptance doesn't mean giving up; it means understanding what is beyond your control and focusing on what is within it.

During the pandemic, people who planned and adapted were the ones who flourished. They accepted the new reality, strategized their lives, and found ways to create meaning in uncertainty. They focused on what was possible rather than what was lost. It wasn't easy, but it was necessary. And the same applies to everyday life. The ability to accept chaos while maintaining clarity is what separates those who crumble under stress from those who rise above it.

One of the simplest ways I learned this was through something as ordinary as traffic. Every day, millions of people find themselves stuck in a seemingly endless line of vehicles, honking, waiting, wasting time. I used to be one of those people—frustrated, impatient, stressed over something entirely out of my hands. Then, I changed my perspective. Instead of resisting the situation, I leaned into it. I started using that time to think, to listen to music, to observe the world around me. Some of the ideas in this book were born in that very traffic, during those moments when I stopped fighting and started embracing the space I was in.

That's the beauty of embracing chaos. When you choose to remain grounded, even the most uncontrollable situations become opportunities for growth and insight. The noise of the world fades, and you are left with a sense of calm clarity, knowing that your peace doesn't depend on the situation, but on how you respond to it.

Chaos is inevitable. Unexpected situations will always arise, plans will change, and things will not always go the way you expect. But what you can control is how you respond. You can choose to meet chaos with frustration, or you can meet it with curiosity, patience, and resilience. The choice is always yours.

And in that very choice, lies the power of intentional decision-making.

Thoughtful Choices

Think of your personal peace like a garden. It's yours to tend to, but it requires attention. External stress, anxieties, and expectations can creep in like weeds, slowly taking over if left unchecked. But when you make intentional choices—what to nurture, what to remove, and what to let go of—you reclaim your space. The same applies to your mind. The way you choose to respond to life's demands determines whether your inner space remains a place of calm or becomes overrun with distractions and unnecessary burdens.

You've likely experienced how easy it is for external factors to disturb your peace. A disagreement, a tight deadline, a comment from someone that lingers in your mind longer than it should. These things happen, but the impact they have on you depends on the choices you make in response. It's not always about eliminating negativity but choosing not to feed it. When you learn to pause, reflect, and decide how much weight you give to a situation, you take back control of your emotional state.

Inner peace is not a distant destination; it's built through the decisions you make every day. Small, intentional choices—choosing kindness over conflict, self-discipline over procrastination, gratitude over complaint—

lay the foundation for a life that feels aligned and steady. Many people seek peace through external means—vacations, material comforts, validation from others—but true peace starts internally, in the thoughts you allow and the actions you take.

I once had a conversation with someone who had been meditating for months but still felt restless. "It's not working," they told me. When we talked further, it became clear why. While they had created a habit of sitting in stillness, they hadn't changed the way they reacted to life outside of that practice. Meditation alone wasn't enough. The real work was in applying that mindfulness to daily situations—choosing patience when frustration arose, staying present instead of overthinking, letting go of what they couldn't control instead of carrying it with them.

Your peace is shaped by your choices. If you want to cultivate it, you have to be intentional. Reflect on the way you respond to stress—how did you handle challenges today? Could you have done anything differently? Small shifts in awareness lead to big transformations over time.

Often, it's situations and misunderstandings that pull people into unnecessary stress. If you approach every interaction with an open mind, assume good intent, and choose not to be weighed down by minor disruptions, you begin to shift the way peace fits into your life.

You have the ability to reset your mind whenever you feel overwhelmed. If the stress builds up, go back to what you've learned in this boo*k. Press Ctrl+Alt+Del a*nd reset.

Let go of what doesn't serve you. Make choices that align with the life you want to live.

Happiness doesn't come from controlling everything around you. It comes from knowing what you can influence, embracing what you cannot, and making thoughtful choices that align with your peace.

It all comes down to this—how you choose to show up for yourself in every moment. The world will move at its own pace, circumstances will shift, and uncertainty will always find its way in. But through it all, you remain. Your choices, your responses, your perspective—these are yours to shape. Every moment offers a chance to step forward with clarity, to release what weighs you down, and to claim the peace that has always been within reach. In the end, control was never about mastering the world around you. It was always about mastering yourself.

Chapter 15

OBSERVATION, IMAGINATION, AND INNOVATION

Happiness doesn't happen by chance or without effort—it's something you build, shape, and nurture over time, as you've likely seen throughout this book. It's not a reward for the lucky or a random moment that comes and goes. Happiness is created, step by step, with care and intention. Some people may stumble upon fleeting moments of joy, but those who experience lasting happiness are the ones who cultivate it deliberately.

It's an art, a practice, and something deeply personal to each of us.

Across cultures, there are countless perspectives on what it means to lead a fulfilling life. In Japan, there's *ikigai*—finding purpose in the intersection of what you love, what you're good at, what the world needs, and what you can be rewarded for. In Denmark, *hygge* reminds us of the joy in life's small comforts and togetherness. In South Africa, *ubuntu* emphasizes shared humanity—the idea that "I am because we are." These traditions remind us that happiness isn't a universal formula; it's a reflection of who we are, where we come from, and how we choose to navigate life. It's shaped by our environment, our routines, and the decisions we make every day.

At its core, happiness is a choice—a choice to seek change, however small, that can lead to a better version of our lives. Think about the last time you made a change in your routine. It could have been as simple as rearranging your workspace, which suddenly made you feel more productive. Or perhaps you approached a tough conversation differently, leading to a more positive outcome than you expected. Maybe you decided to start your mornings with a walk or some quiet time, and before you knew it, your entire day felt lighter.

What led you to make that shift? Chances are, you noticed something wasn't working, you imagined how it could be better, and then you found a way to improve it. Without realizing it, you followed a process that has shaped human progress for centuries—*Observation, Imagination, and Innovation.*

Think of the simplest things around you. A chair, for instance. At its core, it is nothing more than a structure to sit on. But over time, people observed how they used it—some needed back support, others needed armrests, and then came the realization that different people needed different heights. With that, chairs evolved. Today, we have reclining chairs, ergonomic chairs, even ones that automatically adjust to posture. The idea wasn't born overnight—it was shaped through keen observation, refined through imagination, and brought to life through innovation.

The same applies to personal happiness. If you observe, imagine, and innovate, your approach to joy will continuously evolve.

Happiness is not one-size-fits-all. It never was. No two people experience it the same way, and yet, we often fall into the trap of looking for a universal formula. But the truth is, happiness is shaped by our unique lives, our environments, and our choices. What makes one person happy might mean nothing to another. That's why the principles of observation, imagination, and innovation are so important—they allow each of us to craft happiness in a way that aligns with who we truly are.

Think about mobile phones. At first, they existed purely for communication. But someone observed that people were carrying cameras, music players, and gaming devices separately. That sparked an idea—what if all those features could be integrated into one device? Today, our phones are more than communication tools; they are our personal assistants, our entertainment hubs, and our windows to the world. That transformation didn't happen randomly—it was driven by observation, imagination, and innovation.

How often do you pause to observe what truly makes you happy?

How much do you allow yourself to imagine a better way to live?

And when was the last time you actively innovated your habits, choices, or routines to create lasting happiness?

As this book comes to a close, the question isn't *'what is happiness?'* but *'how will you shape yours?'* The principles of Observation, Imagination, and Innovation offer you the tools to keep growing, adapting, and refining your life in a way that feels meaningful to you.

The Three Principles

Throughout this book, we've explored countless ways to nurture and sustain happiness. But as we've emphasized, happiness isn't a fixed destination you arrive at and settle into—it's a lifelong journey, an evolving process of growth, reflection, and intentional effort. The happiest people don't stumble upon joy and cling to it, hoping it never fades. Instead, they consistently refine their understanding of what brings them fulfillment, adapt to life's inevitable changes, and actively shape their happiness over time.

Observation, Imagination, and Innovation are the tools that make this possible.

They help us understand where we are, envision where we want to be, and take action to create a life that aligns with our deepest values. These three principles aren't limited to groundbreaking discoveries or revolutionary ideas—they are the foundation of everyday growth, shaping the way we experience the world and how we engage with it.

Happiness, when viewed through this lens, becomes less about chasing fleeting moments of bliss and more about cultivating a dynamic, ever-changing state of balance and contentment. It's not about perfection or an unbroken streak of positivity—it's about resilience, curiosity, and an openness to growth.

Observation: The Foundation of Growth

Everything begins with seeing clearly. But most people go through life reacting rather than observing. We often fail to notice patterns—in ourselves, in others, in our surroundings. Without conscious observation, we repeat the same mistakes, overlook opportunities, and allow life to slip into autopilot. Think about how often we rush through daily routines without really noticing them. Have you ever sat at a traffic signal, impatiently waiting for the light to turn green, only to realize later that you don't even remember the drive? Or found yourself scrolling endlessly on your phone, consuming content but not really absorbing anything?

These small moments reveal a larger truth: when we stop paying attention, life moves past us in a blur.

But when we make observation a habit, we gain insight, clarity, and a deeper understanding of what truly matters.

Think about stand-up comedians. The best ones don't invent jokes out of thin air. They observe life—family interactions, social norms, cultural quirks—and find humor in the details. The power of their comedy isn't in making things up; it's in noticing what others overlook. The same principle applies to happiness. If you don't observe yourself, how will you ever understand what truly brings you joy? What habits make you feel alive? What drains your energy? What environments uplift you, and which ones weigh you down? Without conscious observation, you remain stuck in old patterns.

Jiddu Krishnamurti, one of India's most timeless philosophers, once said:

"The mind has to be in a state when it can see, observe. In that, there is no duality. The mind is simply aware."

These words hold a mirror to the essence of true observation—a delicate art that requires stepping outside the self, letting go of the filters we unconsciously use to interpret the world. Observation, in its purest form, is not about judgment or reaction but about seeing things as they truly are, untouched by personal fears, desires, or expectations. It is simply cultivating a mind that is still but not stagnant, attentive yet unburdened by the noise of internal dialogue.

In many ways, this practice mirrors the spiritual traditions of India, where the act of seeing—"darshan"—is an integral aspect of self-awareness. Whether it is the symbolic act of gazing upon a deity in a temple or the mindful observation of one's breath in meditation, the process begins with surrendering the egoic lens through which we tend to view the world. To truly observe is to dissolve the duality between the observer and the observed, to move beyond the boundaries of "me" and "mine" into a realm of impartial clarity.

When we incorporate this philosophy into our lives, it can be truly transformative.

Instead of criticizing or suppressing your thoughts, imagine simply observing them to understand them as they are. You might notice recurring patterns in how you respond to challenges or recognize how certain fears influence your decisions. This awareness isn't about judging yourself—it's about learning more about who you are. Every moment of mindful observation reveals the space between who you are now and who you want to become.

In this space of non-judgmental awareness, growth becomes possible. By observing without clinging or resisting, you break free from the constant cycle of reacting. Like a river gradually shaping stone, this practice refines you over time. It shows you that the gap between "what is" and "what could be" isn't something to fear but a journey to embrace.

Real growth doesn't come from forcing change but from seeing clearly. Change begins when you can look inward with the same curiosity and openness you'd use to admire a vast, untouched landscape. In that stillness of simple observation, the seeds of transformation quietly begin to grow.

Imagination: The Power to See Beyond the Present

Observation gives you the raw material. But imagination is what transforms it into something meaningful. It allows you to see beyond limitations and explore possibilities. Where do you want to be? What kind of life do you want to create? How can you shift your habits to bring more meaning into your days?

This idea resonates deeply when you think about the visionaries who redefined what was possible. Take Walt Disney, for example. He didn't just create cartoons—he imagined a world where animated characters came to life, where storytelling transcended static drawings to become a fully immersive experience.

Or consider Steve Jobs, who envisioned a phone that wasn't just a tool for making calls, but a device that became an integral part of everyday life, shaping how we communicate, work, and experience the world. These weren't arbitrary ideas that fell into their laps. They were born out of a profound ability to observe, to dream beyond the constraints of the present, and to reimagine what the future could look like.

This same principle of imagination applies to happiness.

For many people, happiness feels like an abstract goal—a vague feeling they hope to achieve someday. "I want to be happy," they'll say, but without really defining what that means. How often do we pause to consider the specifics of what happiness looks like for us? Is it tied to the warmth of relationships, the excitement of meaningful work, the peace of solitude, or perhaps a mix of all three?

Without the ability to imagine happiness in tangible terms, it remains an elusive concept, always just out of reach.

The happiest people don't stumble into joy by accident. They actively design it. They take the time to dream, but not in some far-fetched or unrealistic way. Instead, they use their imagination to connect deeply with their own desires, aspirations, and values. They design their lives in ways that align with what truly matters to them. For some, this might mean prioritizing time for creative pursuits or nurturing relationships that bring them fulfillment. For others, it could mean rethinking their routines, identifying areas that drain their energy, and replacing them with habits that spark joy.

So, take a moment to reflect on your own life. And all that we've discovered so far.

If you could design your perfect day from start to finish, what would it include? What small moments would bring you the most joy?

What do you wish you had more of in your daily routine? Is it laughter, calmness, adventure, or connection?

What's one small change you could make today—a single step that could bring you just a little closer to the life you want to lead?

These questions aren't just exercises; they are acts of imagination in practice.

The happiest people don't sit back and wait for happiness to find them. They explore possibilities. They dare to look beyond what feels obvious or practical and give themselves permission to dream. Even small shifts in perspective or action can open doors to a richer, more meaningful existence.

Imagination isn't about escaping reality—it's about rethinking it.

It's about reshaping your current circumstances to create space for a better version of yourself and your life. When we use imagination not as a fantasy but as a tool for designing change, we allow ourselves to step out of limitations and into something bigger. Happiness, after all, is something we craft, refine, and continually pursue through the stories we tell ourselves and the actions we take.

Innovation: Turning Ideas Into Action

Once you've observed and imagined, the final step is to act.

Happiness, much like any other pursuit in life, thrives on experimentation. What brought you joy five years ago might no longer fulfill you today, and that's okay. We're not static beings; we grow, we change, and so do our needs and desires. The happiest people aren't those with perfect lives, but those who continuously refine their habits, thoughts, and routines to align with their evolving selves.

Innovation isn't confined to technology or science—it's a mindset that applies just as much to personal growth, relationships, and the ways we engage with the world. Think about how companies adapt and evolve to stay relevant: Mobile phones began as tools for simple calls, then expanded to include text messaging, then cameras, and now AI-powered assistants that can manage entire aspects of our lives. Music has transitioned from vinyl records to cassette tapes, then CDs, and now streaming platforms that bring entire libraries to your fingertips. Even food culture evolves—what was once considered "exotic" is now mainstream; sushi, tacos, and kimchi are staples in many households worldwide.

Happiness works the same way. If your daily routines no longer bring you joy, innovate them. Change something. Experiment. See what works and what doesn't. Small, consistent adjustments lead to meaningful transformations over time.

Struggling with stress? Try a new morning routine. Feeling stagnant? Learn a new skill. Drained by negativity? Limit your exposure to toxic news and energy-draining people.

The happiest people are not those who rigidly hold onto old ways of thinking, but those who are willing to adapt, evolve, and reshape their lives to stay aligned with what matters most to them. Innovation is the key to breaking free from stagnant habits, from outdated beliefs, and from routines that no longer serve you. It's about actively creating the conditions for happiness rather than waiting for them to appear.

And that's why I say, it is important to have a true sense of observation, imagination, and innovation for a happy life. The principles we've explored here are not merely abstract ideas—they are tools. Use them. Apply them. Make them part of your daily experience, and happiness will no longer feel like something to chase, but something you create, every single day.

Observation in Action

Now that we've explored the three principles, let's take a closer look at how observation plays out in real life. Happiness is not a mystery, nor is it entirely personal. While each person experiences joy in their own way, patterns emerge when we pay close attention to those who seem truly content.

The challenge is to observe without comparing, to learn without feeling the need to measure up. When we engage in deep observation, we begin to notice the habits, perspectives, and choices that contribute to lasting happiness.

One of the simplest ways to understand happiness is to study people who embody it—not the ones who merely appear happy in photographs or social media, but those who radiate contentment in their everyday lives. Think of that one person in your life who always seems at ease. They don't necessarily have the most wealth, the best career, or an easy life. Yet, they move through challenges with grace, bringing warmth to those around them. What do they do differently?

From years of observation, a few common traits stand out. Happy people tend to be kind without expecting anything in return. They appreciate small joys instead of waiting for grand moments. They avoid blaming others when things go wrong and focus on what they can control. They remain curious, always seeking to learn and grow. They adapt to changes instead of resisting them. They are self-aware, grounded, and able to find balance in their emotions. Most importantly, they uplift others—they take joy in the happiness and success of those around them.

Take a moment to reflect. Think about the happiest people you know. What is it about them that draws others in? Is it their ability to remain calm under pressure? Their habit of making people feel valued? Their resilience in the face of setbacks? More often than not, their happiness isn't the result of external achievements but of how they engage with life itself. It is not limited to grand gestures but is often rooted in the smallest choices—choosing gratitude over complaint, kindness over frustration, and patience over reaction.

Happiness isn't an accident—it is a practice. And one of the best ways to learn is through true observation. The key, however, is to observe without falling into the trap of comparison. Two people can adopt the same habits and still experience different results. Your happiness is your own journey, not a race against anyone else's.

Purushottam Laxman Deshpande, one of India's most beloved writers, once said:

"Who is saying is more important than what is being said."

This quote highlights how people often give more weight to who is sharing an idea rather than the idea itself. For example, if a thought leader shares a perspective, it may gain widespread attention, while the same idea shared by an ordinary person might go unnoticed. The flip side is that once someone is taken for granted, even their most valuable insights can be overlooked simply because they are no longer considered important.

As you observe, filter what applies to you and let go of what does not. Learn from happy people, but don't try to replicate their lives. Instead, adapt their insights into your own world, shaping them to fit your values and circumstances. Each person's path is different, and true happiness is found in embracing your own journey while learning from others.

Learning from others also means paying attention to the subtle behaviors that contribute to lasting happiness. Have you noticed how some people greet strangers with warmth, making small gestures that brighten someone else's day? How they listen attentively without rushing to respond? How they choose kindness even when no one is watching? These small acts, repeated over time, build a foundation for happiness that goes beyond momentary pleasure.

Look around you, and you'll find examples of small yet meaningful acts of kindness everywhere—offering a glass of water to a guest, helping a stranger in need, or sharing food with a neighbor—reflect a deeply ingrained cultural belief that joy multiplies when shared.

There is wisdom in everyday life.

When you observe closely, you start to notice patterns in your own behavior and the behavior of those around you. The mind becomes sharper, more aware, more engaged.

Observations bring clarity, and clarity leads to change.

The more you refine your ability to observe, the more you uncover ways to cultivate happiness that align with your true self. And sometimes, happiness is found in the simplest moments—watching the rain from your balcony, sipping a cup of chai with a loved one, or sharing a laugh over a childhood memory.

As you go through your day, take a moment to pause and observe. Who are the happiest people in your life? Can you name them? What do they prioritize? How do they respond to challenges? And most importantly, what can you take from these observations and apply to your own life?

When you engage with the world as an active participant rather than a passive observer, you open yourself to continuous growth and learning. Small shifts in awareness can lead to profound changes in how you experience life.

In the end, happiness is not something to be chased. It is something to be created, shaped, and refined. And it all begins with the ability to observe with clarity, awareness, and an open heart. The more you pay attention, the more you realize that happiness is already present in the moments you choose to value. The key is to slow down, notice, and appreciate what is already around you—because more often than not, the happiness you seek is hidden in the life you are already living.

The Power of Imagination

Once you've trained yourself to observe with clarity, the next step is to expand beyond what is and step into what could be. Imagination is where raw observations turn into possibilities, where the ordinary transforms into something greater. Without imagination, the world remains static, unchanged. But with it, progress happens—both in the external world and within ourselves.

Think about the most transformative ideas in history. Every invention, every work of art, every societal change began as a thought—an unseen possibility that someone had the courage to explore. A child dreams of building a castle long before they have the tools to do so. An entrepreneur envisions a solution to a problem before they create a product. A musician hears a melody before it is ever played. Happiness, too, follows this pattern. If you cannot see it in your mind, how will you create it in your life?

Imagination is often mistaken for wishful thinking, but it is far more than that.

It is an active process, a skill that shapes reality.

Albert Einstein once said, "Imagination is more important than knowledge. Knowledge is limited. Imagination encircles the world." Knowledge tells us how things work. Imagination allows us to reimagine what they could become. Without imagination, we remain confined to what already exists, unable to reach for something better.

Think about the computer mouse, something so small yet so essential in our daily lives. Before its invention, interacting with computers was cumbersome, requiring complex commands. But Douglas Engelbart imagined a device that could simplify the process—a simple, intuitive way for users to control a screen. Today, we hardly think about it, but our interactions with technology would be completely different if he hadn't allowed himself to think beyond what was in front of him.

The same principle applies to happiness. If you are constantly waiting for happiness to arrive, treating it as something that will happen once everything is perfect, you will always be waiting.

Instead, what if you treated happiness like something you could design? What if you took the time to imagine a version of your life where you felt fulfilled, energized, and at peace? The happiest people do not passively wait for joy; they visualize it, shape it, and move toward it with intention.

Happiness is often thought of as something external—an outcome of circumstances.

But if you look closer, it is driven by how we see the world. Imagine two people in the same situation—one sees a problem, the other sees an opportunity. One sees hardship, the other sees a lesson. The difference lies not in what happens to them, but in how they perceive and respond to it. This is the power of imagination in action. It allows us to reshape our experiences and create a sense of purpose, even in the face of challenges

Now, let's apply this to our own lives. When was the last time you truly imagined a better way of being? Not in a vague, daydreaming way, but with clarity and intention? If you could design a perfect day, what would it look like? What brings you energy? What routines or habits drain you? When you take the time to reflect, you begin to see opportunities to shape your own happiness. Visualizing the life you want is the first step in making it a reality.

At work, people often chase promotions and pay raises, believing these will bring happiness. But in reality, what creates fulfillment is deeper than financial success. Recognition, trust, a sense of belonging—these often matter more in the long run. What if, instead of focusing solely on external rewards, you imagined ways to bring more meaning into your daily routine? Small shifts—choosing to work on projects that excite you, building stronger relationships with colleagues, or finding ways to challenge yourself—can completely change your experience.

So, how do you strengthen your imagination?

Like any muscle, it grows with use. Read widely. Engage with different perspectives. Tell stories. Ask questions. Be curious. The more you expose yourself to ideas, the more you stretch your ability to see beyond the present.

Happiness is something you have the power design.

The more vividly you can see your ideal life, the more likely you are to build it.

Innovating for Joy

Adapting habits and perspectives is the key to creating a life of lasting fulfillment. But how do you turn insights into meaningful change? How do you move from simply observing and imagining to truly living the life you aspire to?

The answer lies in innovation—not the kind limited to science, technology, or businesses, but the kind that builds a bridge between where you are now and where you want to be. It's about taking what you've learned, your observations and ideas, and applying them in ways that continuously elevate your life.

Too often, we think of innovation as something reserved for inventors or entrepreneurs, but it's so much more than that.

At its core, innovation is a mindset—a willingness to experiment, to challenge the status quo, and to pursue growth with intention. And it's absolutely essential for personal happiness.

The happiest people don't sit back and wait for change to come to them. They create it. They take ownership of their lives, constantly refining how they approach their days and the challenges they face.

Think about it—innovation can show up in the smallest, most personal ways. It might mean redesigning your morning routine to fuel your energy and focus for the day ahead. It could mean rethinking how you nurture your relationships, finding new ways to connect and communicate with the people who matter most. It could even mean exploring deeper meaning in your work, shifting perspectives or habits to align your career with your values and passions.

The beauty of innovation is that it's not about big, sweeping changes. It's about micro-adjustments, small but intentional improvements that compound over time. It's about trying, failing, learning, and trying again. The happiest people aren't those who never face challenges or setbacks— they're the ones who see those moments as opportunities to innovate, to adapt, and to grow stronger.

When you stop innovating, you stop growing.

Growth isn't a destination; it's an ongoing process of curiosity, creativity, and courage. So, ask yourself: What small but meaningful changes can you make today? How can you take the insights you've gathered and transform them into action? In the end, it's not just about where you want to go—it's about the journey of getting there, and the person you become along the way.

Consider how life around you has changed. A few decades ago, communication was limited to letters or expensive long-distance calls. Today, with a few taps on a screen, we can connect with loved ones anywhere in the world. But this didn't happen overnight. Someone observed a need, imagined a solution, and then innovated to make it a reality. The same principle applies to happiness. What aspects of your life feel outdated or unfulfilling? What small changes could lead to a better experience?

Innovation isn't about grand reinventions—it's about consistent, meaningful shifts.

If your daily habits don't bring you joy, adjust them.

If your approach to relationships feels unbalanced, rethink how you engage with others.

If work feels monotonous, introduce variety into your routine.

Growth happens when you continuously refine the way you live, aligning it with your evolving needs and aspirations.

We often think of happiness as something we either have or don't have. But happiness is more like a habit—one that requires regular maintenance. The small things you do daily, the habits you cultivate, and the thoughts you entertain shape your overall sense of well-being.

Think about people who keep journals to track their thoughts, goals, or gratitude. This simple habit helps them stay self-aware and adjust their mindset over time. Some people practice mindfulness, others engage in creative pursuits, and some prioritize spending time with people who uplift them. These aren't random acts—they are intentional innovations designed to support long-term happiness.

If you want to be happier, don't wait for a perfect moment—start by making small changes today. Try a new way of organizing your day. Experiment with different ways to unwind after work. Introduce a habit that encourages self-growth. The more you engage with the process of improvement, the more fulfilled you become.

Happiness requires movement.

If you feel stuck in old routines, old patterns of thinking, or habits that no longer serve you, it's a sign that innovation is needed. Many people resist change, fearing the uncertainty it brings, but in doing so, they also resist growth.

Take a look at your life right now. Where do you feel uninspired? What routines have become dull? Where do you feel drained? Instead of settling into patterns that don't serve you, challenge yourself to shake things up. Learn something new. Change your approach to a recurring problem. Be open to exploring possibilities you hadn't considered before.

Albert Szent-Györgyi, a Hungarian biochemist, once said:

"Innovation is seeing what everybody has seen and thinking what nobody has thought."

The happiest people aren't those who have the most; they are those who see opportunities where others see limitations. They take what life offers and turn it into something meaningful. They don't wait for joy to arrive—they innovate ways to create it.

But beware- innovation isn't a one-time act; it's a lifelong mindset. The world around us is constantly evolving, and so are we. Like I said, what brought you happiness a few years ago may no longer feel fulfilling today. That's okay. Growth means recognizing when it's time to adapt.

Be a student of your own happiness. Keep learning, keep experimenting, and keep refining the way you approach life. Stay curious about what brings you joy and be willing to adjust your course when needed. The most content people are those who embrace change rather than resist it.

As you move forward, think about the ways you can innovate your own happiness. What small habits can you change? What perspectives can you shift? How can you refine the way you experience life? The answers lie not in waiting for happiness to happen but in taking the steps to create it, one thoughtful change at a time.

Your Happiness, Your Creation

There comes a moment—sometimes small, sometimes life-changing—when you realize that happiness isn't something you need to chase. If this book helped you reach that realization, great. If it came from your own life, even better. Either way, remember this: happiness isn't something far off, waiting behind a future goal, a perfect situation, or someone else's approval. It's always been here, shaped by the choices you make every day.

Think back to where we began. Maybe you picked up this book looking for answers, a guide to a happier life. Maybe you were searching for clarity, a way to break free from old habits that weren't serving you. But what if the truth was never about finding happiness, but about making it? What if, all along, the power to create a meaningful, fulfilling life was already in your hands?

Look at the patterns in your life. The days that felt light, effortless. The moments when you lost track of time, fully present in what you were doing. The conversations that left you feeling seen, understood. The simple, ordinary joys—a morning walk, a shared meal, the way the sky looks after it rains. These are not accidents. These are the results of what you choose to focus on, what you choose to nurture, what you choose to let go of.

Happiness is not a formula. It is not a straight path. It is a rhythm, a constant process of observing, imagining, and innovating. The happiest people aren't the ones with perfect lives; they are the ones who continue shaping their world, adapting to change, and making space for joy in the way that feels right for them.

So, what now? What do you do when you reach the last page?

You begin again.

You wake up tomorrow and notice. You pay attention to what makes you feel alive. You imagine a life that excites you, and then, step by step, you make it real. You try, you fail, you adjust. You let go of what no longer fits, and you create something better. You stop waiting for happiness to arrive, and you start crafting it, piece by piece, in the way only you can.

Because happiness is not something you find.

It is something you build.

And now, you know how.